SpringerBriefs in Law

SpringerBriefs present concise summaries of cutting-edge research and practical applications across a wide spectrum of fields. Featuring compact volumes of 50 to 125 pages, the series covers a range of content from professional to academic. Typical topics might include:

- A timely report of state-of-the art analytical techniques
- A bridge between new research results, as published in journal articles, and a contextual literature review
- A snapshot of a hot or emerging topic
- A presentation of core concepts that students must understand in order to make independent contributions

SpringerBriefs in Law showcase emerging theory, empirical research, and practical application in Law from a global author community. SpringerBriefs are characterized by fast, global electronic dissemination, standard publishing contracts, standardized manuscript preparation and formatting guidelines, and expedited production schedules.

Luiz Guilherme Marinoni

Culture and Predictability of Law

A Justification from a Modern Historical Perspective

Springer

Luiz Guilherme Marinoni
Constitutional Law and Procedural Law
Federal University of Paraná
Curitiba, Paraná, Brazil

ISSN 2192-855X ISSN 2192-8568 (electronic)
SpringerBriefs in Law
ISBN 978-3-031-87160-3 ISBN 978-3-031-87161-0 (eBook)
https://doi.org/10.1007/978-3-031-87161-0

Translation from the Portuguese language edition: "A Ética dos Precedentes" by Luiz Guilherme Marinoni, © Author 2024. Published by Thomson Reuters Revista dos Tribunais. All Rights Reserved.

This Springer imprint is published by the registered company Springer Nature Switzerland AG
The registered company address is: Gewerbestrasse 11, 6330 Cham, Switzerland

Contents

About the Author

Luiz Guilherme Marinoni is a Master and Doctor of Laws from the Catholic University of São Paulo, with a postdoctoral degree from Università di Milano; a visiting scholar at Columbia University and Fordham University; an honorary member of the Presidium of the International Association of Procedural Law and president of the Brazilian Association of Constitutional Procedural Law; professor at the Federal University of Paraná, former federal prosecutor and former president of the Brazilian Bar Association, Curitiba; a consultant for the Brazilian House of Representatives on the Brazilian Civil Procedural Code and the Brazilian Constitutional Procedural Code projects; and an international consultant for the project *Principles of Transnational Civil Procedure* (American Law Institute and UNIDROIT).Marinoni is the author of several books published in Brazil, Chile, Colombia, Italy, Mexico, Peru, Portugal and Spain and of numerous articles published in prominent journals in Argentina, Bolivia, Brazil, Chile, China, Colombia, El Salvador, Germany, Italy, Mexico, Peru, Poland, Portugal, South Korea, Spain and Uruguay. Marinoni is the winner of the 2009 and 2017 Jabuti Prize and a finalist in the 2007, 2010 and 2015 prizes.

Chapter 1
Introduction

Contents

This book, calling on the Weberian idea of rational law and by drawing on the renowned *Protestant Ethic and the Spirit of Capitalism*,[1] seeks to demonstrate that formal legal rationality, proper to European continental law of the late nineteenth century and early twentieth century, has a distinct "protestant ethic" component, more precisely of Calvinistic values—which, as we know, were also present at the English Revolution of 1688 (the Glorious Revolution) and, soon after, were at the basis for the creation of the Constitution of the United States.[2] The religious values that determined the protestant way of life, which led to the development of capitalism, demanded a rational and predictable law, expressed by the scope and clarity that were peculiar to scientific positivism or the German conceptualism of the beginning of the twentieth century.[3]

English common law, which Weber saw as devoid of formal rationality, because it did not support generalization and comprehensiveness, has become a predictable system through *stare decisis*, which shows not only that it is not the same as common law, but especially to enlighten that binding precedent is necessary as law strays further from calculability.

The transformation of civil law due to the impact of constitutionalism, the increasingly widespread use of general clauses and the evolution of interpretation theory eliminated logical positivism's pretensions and, as a consequence, the predictability upon which it would be attainable. However, if the law contemplated by Weber ceased to exist and the new law has come to depend largely on the subjectivity of the judge, it does not mean that society has become helpless and deposed of

[1] Weber (2004a, b).

[2] Levinson (1988), Wood (1998), and Martínez (2003).

[3] Weber (1996, 2004a, b).

L. G. Marinoni, *Culture and Predictability of Law*, SpringerBriefs in Law,
https://doi.org/10.1007/978-3-031-87161-0_1

the guarantees of predictability and equality, as if the new profile of civil law could not be matched with a consistent legal order and a rational distribution of justice.

I have also considered in the book the effects of the values of Tridentine Catholicism on the colonization of Brazil and especially the Weberian concept of patrimonialism from Sérgio Buarque de Holanda's perspective to demonstrate its significance in the relationship between the Brazilian people and their government. Patriarchy and patrimonialism, particular features in the formative process of Brazilian culture, gave rise to the Buarquean concept of the "cordial man",[4] who, accustomed to the intimate environment and the exchange of family favours, transforms public space into private and, precisely because he cannot bear impersonality and rationality, sees the law as something that should be bypassed by the aid of the "patrimonial official",[5] i.e. the official who works for the executive or the judiciary branches of government only for his own benefit.

We should point out, from the outset, that it is not very difficult to establish a clear connection between a culture that sustains, without any embarrassment, the possibility of a man resisting the law that harms him by using his relationships and a system that echoes the lack of unity in solving similar cases and that sees the uneven treatment of people as something natural. In this way, the lack of reaction to a judicial system that denies equality and predictability may well unveil the interests of various social settings, including groups of judges and a share of lawyers.

Personalism, another feature of our cultural heritage, made up an obstacle to social cohesion that could be pointed out as a cause of the well-known lukewarmness of our institutions. The absence of institutionalism in some of our judges is backed by the exaltation of autonomy and individualism, albeit masquerading them as "freedom to judge" and "exclusive submission to the law". Nor is it impossible to see from here that a judge who has no commitment to overall objectives cannot understand that adjudication depends on several other functions, one of which is to assign meaning to the law through binding precedent.

At the end, we seek to demonstrate the fundamentality of precedent for the unity and the development of the law, clarity and generality, the promotion of equality, institutional strengthening, the limitation of State power, predictability, economic rationality, respect for the law and the increase of personal responsibility.

The justification, or rather the ethicization of precedent, in addition to being related to all these factors, implies that respect for precedent is an indispensable way to preserve the values of the rule of law, as well as to facilitate a way of life in which the law assumes its due dignity, in that, besides being applied equitably, it can determine behaviours and generate a way of life marked by personal responsibility.

---

[4] Holanda (1995, 2012).

[5] The category of the "patrimonial official", credited to Max Weber, is used by Sérgio Buarque de Holanda. To the "patrimonial" official, political governance itself is presented as a subject of his own personal interest; functions, jobs and benefits that he earns from it are related to the personal rights of the employee and not to objective interests, as in a true bureaucratic state, where the specialization of functions and the efforts to ensure legal guarantees for citizens prevail. Holanda (1995), p. 146.

To lead a life based on law—a personal ethic of respect for the law regardless of the consequences of its inobservance—and for it to have enough strength to regulate life, it requires unity, and therefore, supreme courts must act as courts of precedent, with which one can stimulate an ethics based on personal responsibility.

References

Holanda SB (1995) Raízes do Brasil. Companhia das Letras
Holanda SB (2012) O Homem Cordial. Companhia das Letras e Penguin Group
Levinson S (1988) Constitutional Faith. Princeton University Press
Martínez FR (2003) La ética protestante y el espíritu del constitucionalismo. Universidad Externado de Colombia
Weber M (1996) Essais de Sociologie des Religions. Gallimard
Weber M (2004a) A ética protestante e o "espírito" do capitalismo. Companhia das Letras
Weber M (2004b) Economia e Sociedade, vol 2. Editora UnB
Wood GS (1998) The Creation of the American Republic: 1776–1787. The University of North Carolina Press

Chapter 2
Protestantism, Capitalism, Rationality of Law and Predictability in Weber: Between the Common Law and Civil Law of the End of the Nineteenth Century

Contents

In this chapter, the author shows that Weber did not identify formal legal rationality with predictability but saw *stare decisis* as a mechanism able of providing predictability in a "formally irrational law", which means that, although the common law does not hold the same kind of rationality as that of the traditional European continental law, it was able to secure, under *stare decisis*, a degree of predictability that allowed the flourishing of capitalism.

2.1 Protestantism, Inner-Worldly Asceticism, Rationality and Capitalism

Between 1904 and 1905, Weber published the two parts of the first version of the classic *The Protestant Ethic and the 'Spirit' of Capitalism*. This first version was, so to speak, "complemented" in 1920—shortly before his death—when he incorporated into the book important additions and robust notes, especially intended to clarify it and to answer his critics.[1]

---

[1] Weber has left us not only two editions of the *Protestant Ethic* but also two different versions: the first one, published in two prints, in 1904 and 1905, and the other, revised and expanded, edited in 1920. All translations that we know today, to begin with the first one, from 1930, signed by Talcott Parsons, were based on the expanded edition from 1920, which was published by Weber in the first volume of the *Essays in Sociology*. There are significant differences between the two versions, given that the second and latter ones received not only small changes and grammatical or termino-

L. G. Marinoni, *Culture and Predictability of Law*, SpringerBriefs in Law,
https://doi.org/10.1007/978-3-031-87161-0_2

Weber's purpose is to demonstrate that the way of life of the Protestant religion, where we find Calvinists, Lutherans, Methodists, Mennonites and Quakers, contributed to the development of capitalism. Initially, the book establishes a relationship between economic progress and protestant peoples, thus demonstrating a clear connection between Protestant and Catholic religious orientations, the choice of occupation and one's subsequent professional destiny.[2] It is reported that Catholics were more interested in the humanistic *Gymnasien*, while Protestants preferred establishments, specially designed to prepare for commercial and industrial professions, that is, for life in business, a phenomenon that could not be explained by the difference in fortunes but that would explain the reduced interest of Catholics in capitalist acquisition. In the second chapter of Part I, Weber makes first reference to what he calls the "spirit" of capitalism. He points to a text by Benjamin Franklin, from which he extracts the idea of "profession as a duty" and "money-making" as the result and expression of skill in a profession. Franklin's maxims, by recommending hard and systematic work, coupled with austerity, synthesize the "spirit of capitalism". It is, according to Weber, an ethics that when violated represents a breach of duty.[3] It is in this cultural context that the now trivial idea of the "profession as a duty" arises, a constitutive element of capitalism.[4] The third chapter refers to the concept of vocation in Luther. It is a concept related to the idea of working as a God-given mission, reflected in the terms *Beruf* and *Calling*. It is intended to show that Protestants, unlike Catholics, rejected monastic asceticism (seen as other-worldly asceticism) as a means of salvation and saw strict compliance with worldly duties as the only way of life that pleased God.[5] The glorification of God, according to Protestantism, should be done through daily practice, not through the seclusion of a monastic life. The duty to exercise one's profession is, in this sense, a consequence of the Reformation, hence the idea of professional vocation in Luther and, more

logical adjustments but also, and most importantly, valuable additions by the author. Pierucci (2005), p. 187.

[2] Catholic artisans show a greater tendency to remain in craftsmanship, therefore becoming master craftsmen with a relatively greater frequency, while Protestants flock to factories, to a relatively greater extent, to occupy the upper echelons of skilled proletariat positions and administrative posts. Weber (2004a, b, c), pp. 32–33.

[3] In effect, here, we are preaching not simply a technique of life but also a peculiar "ethic" whose violation is treated not merely as folly but also as a kind of failure to fulfil one's duty: this, above all, is the essence of the matter. What is taught here is not just "business acumen"—something that is found quite frequently—but also an ethos that expresses itself, and it is precisely in this capacity that interests us (id. p. 45).

[4] See id. p. 47.

[5] The concept of *Beruf* expresses the central dogma of all Protestant denominations who condemn the Catholic division of moral imperatives in *pracepta* and *consilia* and who recognize that the only way of life that pleases God is not in supplanting worldly morality with monastic asceticism, but, instead, is solely in compliance with inner-worldly duties, as they stem from an individual's position in life, which, exactly for this reason, become this individual's professional calling. Id. p. 72.

precisely, the relationship between a way of life influenced by Protestantism—especially by Calvinism—and the "spirit" of capitalism.[6]

In Part II, Weber examines, in the first chapter, the religious foundations of inner-worldly asceticism, i.e. the values of the Protestant religion that led to the idea that devotion to God must be shown by practices and behaviours that are part of every-day life, such as the search for perfection in one's profession. Inner-worldly asceticism presupposes that work is a religious duty that must be exercised with strict discipline, which characterizes the ideal means for Christians to realize, in the "inner world", the desire of God. It is in this sense that Weber speaks of "ascetic Protestantism" and cautiously considers the content of the core values of Calvinism, pietism, Methodism and Anabaptist movements to highlight and define the religious foundations of inner-worldly asceticism. Hence, Weber warns, referring to Calvinism, that the doctrine of predestination—that no act done by man can influence salvation, all men being convicted or elected by a divine decree—is a dogmatic foundation of the puritan morality of a conduct of life methodically rationalized. Weber demonstrates that Calvinism rejected the sacramental means of salvation proper to Catholicism, especially salvation by works and confession, and focused on inner-worldly conduct, specifically professional work, means of action that would give Calvinists proof of their election.[7] The concern with the correctness of behaviour and with the proper performance of daily tasks, which Calvinists needed to *prove* for their salvation, has stimulated the *methodical control* in the conduct of lives. According to Weber, this *rationalization* of the conduct of life in the world while keeping an eye on the "other world" is the result of ascetic Protestantism's concept of profession.[8]

In the last chapter, Weber relates ascetic Protestantism to the "spirit" of capitalism. He demonstrates that taking work as a religious duty, as a means to prove faith and the election of oneself, was a powerful propellant of a life marked by the capitalist "spirit". This systematic and continuous work, from which profits naturally arise, contributed to the development of capitalism precisely because it signifies a proper way to glorify God *inside* the world. Profit would be the result of a

[6] It was reformed education, in effect, that first proclaimed that professional activity and social function had not only moral but also essentially religious value. What pleases God is not the asceticism of monks but, quite on the contrary, the conscientious exercise of all professional and secular activities that man performs in his daily life. It is through the meticulous execution of these profane tasks, to which man is called by God, that they become the object of his vocation. Biéler (2012), p. 586.

[7] And, on the other hand, professional work without rest stands out as the most prominent means of achieving this self-confidence. He, and only he, would dispel religious doubt and give certainty to the state of grace. Weber (2004a, b, c), p. 102.

[8] And this ascesis was no longer an *opus supererogationis* but a feat required of anyone who wanted to assure themselves of their blessedness. This singular life of saints, demanded by religion and distinct from natural life, took place—and this is decisive—no longer outside the world in monastic communities but within the world and its orders. This rationalization of the conduct of life while having an eye on the Other World is the effect of ascetic Protestantism's concept of profession (id. p. 139).

systematic conduct of life, including work, and in this way would be an appropriate way to praise God. But Protestant asceticism not only broke the shackles that inhibited profit, but it also condemned the relaxed enjoyment of possessions, strangling frivolous consumption, especially luxury consumption, which resulted, in Weber's words, in the accumulation of capital through the *ascetic compulsion to save*.[9]

The relationship between asceticism, especially derived from Calvinism, and the "spirit" of capitalism involves the rationalization of human conduct. Inner-worldly asceticism or the performance of work as a religious duty is not only clearly linked to the rationalization of life-leading control, but it is also a rational way of seeing salvation, inasmuch as it, for believers in the doctrine of predestination, could never depend on magical or sacramental means—referred to as "works"—but only require *proof* through the *rational* control of professional performance or actions of inner-worldly life.

The repudiation of the sacraments, seen as magic, and the idea that only perseverance in behaviour directed towards the glorification of God or towards the search for signs of election had meaning, led Weber, in the second version of *The Protestant Ethic and the "Spirit" of Capitalism*, to point to the "disenchantment of the world". Weber refers to a historical process of demagification of salvation and, thus, to the rationalization of life in the West.[10] As Pierucci explains, "disenchantment" and "ethicization-moralization" are two sides of the same coin or two faces of the same historical-religious process that characterizes the direction followed by social and cultural rationalization of the West, a process in which rationalization is experienced as rational work.[11]

The disenchantment of the world or the demagification of salvation are related to inner-worldly asceticism and the exercise of labour, which are both permeated by protestant values, which led to a form of rational and end-oriented life. It is a peculiar form of rationalization, coming from religious values. Therefore, it is certain

[9] Inner-worldly Protestant asceticism—to summarize what has been said so far—acted in this way, with all vehemence, against the relaxed enjoyment of possessions; it strangled consumption, especially luxury consumption. In compensation, it had the psychological effect of freeing enrichment from the obstacles of traditionalist ethics, breaking the chains that surrounded the ambition for profit, not only by legalizing it but also by viewing it (in the sense described) as directly willed by God. And now, by comparing that strangling of consumption with this unobstructed desire for profit, the result is evident: the accumulation of capital through ascetic coercion to saving (ibidem pp. 155–157).

[10] As explained by Pierucci, one of the most important Weberians of the last decades, the term disenchantment, understood as demagification, takes on the dimension of a great historical process that is specifically ethical-religious and specifically Western and thus intends to designate, almost as a proper and non-common name, the very long period of peculiar religious rationalization through which, thanks to purely historical reasons (*rein historisch*), Western religiosity passed under the cultural hegemony achieved by this form of "characteristically moralized" monotheistic faith, the repressor of universal magic, called Judeo-Christianity. Its creators and first bearers (*Träger*) were the prophets of Israel, the flower of ancient Judaism, and the Protestant sects were its radical and self-confident carriers (*Träger*) in the heroic time of the cultural birth of the modern civilization of work, its religious destination. Pierucci (2005), p. 199.

[11] Id. p. 206.

that one cannot think of disenchantment as (synonymous with) rationalization, as if the latter could not have other sources or intensities or, even, as if rationalization operated by the disenchantment of the world was not a particular rationalization of the way of life largely due to a specific reason. This is because the process of rationalization, as Weber points out, takes place differently in different spheres of social life.

As we know, the content of Calvinism is strongly influenced by the doctrine of predestination, as put in the Westminster Confession, 1647, which records that "By the decree of God, for the manifestation of His glory, some men and angels are predestinated unto everlasting life; and others foreordained to everlasting death" (Chapter III, n. 3) and "Those of mankind that are predestinated unto life, God, before the foundation of the world was laid, according to His eternal and immutable purpose, and the secret counsel and good pleasure of His will, has chosen, in Christ, unto everlasting glory, out of His mere free grace and love, without any foresight of faith, or good works, or perseverance in either of them, or any other thing in the creature, as conditions, or causes moving Him thereunto; and all to the praise of His glorious grace" (Chapter III, n. 5).

Calvinists, by accepting the doctrine that certain men were elected or saved before mankind came into the world, could not seek salvation in their life, whether by works or sacraments, but could only try to find the *evidence* that they had been elected by God.[12] Weber questions how it was possible to support this doctrine in a time when the "other world" was more important and, in many aspects, also safer than the interests of life in this world.[13] As the uncertainty of election generated extreme distress, Weber cautions that professional work without rest was distinguished as the most salient means to achieve self-confidence in election, seen as the only way to dispel religious doubt and to give certainty of the state of grace.

As systematic work helps in proving election, it is natural that a strong emphasis on personal responsibility ensues from it. Calvinists, because they feel the weight of the "duty of the profession", cannot fail to perform its inherent obligations. There is not only the duty to properly execute the "professional mission" but also the duty to fulfil the obligations that stem from its exercise. To neglect the rigorous and continuous exercise of the profession and to not pay a debt are both evidence of the absence of election. The exercise of a profession and the fulfilment of obligations as a religious duty foster within Calvinists an extreme strictness with themselves, that is, a rigorous and continuous inspection of their professional and personal conduct.

---

[12] What—in the countries where capitalism and culture were most developed, the Netherlands, England and France of the sixteenth and seventeenth centuries—characterized, in the most typical fashion, the Calvinist churches and sects, at a time when they were most ardently opposed, is their dogma of predestination. It is around this dogma that the most violent ecclesiastical struggles were fought during the seventeenth and eighteenth centuries; it is, therefore, what must be considered the most specific dogma of the Calvinist faith. It is this dogma that gives meaning to all acts of life for a reformist (says Weber), even those that seem meaningless. Man lives not for himself but only to honour God, the lone sovereign, whose decrees determine the entire history of humanity and decide the salvation of each individual. Biéler (2012), p. 100.

[13] Weber (2004a, b, c), p. 100.

The evidence of election, because it had nothing to do with doing good works in isolation, i.e. works for salvation,[14] required a continuous and systematic self-inspection, capable of providing Calvinists "certainty" that they had been elected.[15]

We should mention, therefore, that the idea of professional duty, with which a strong emphasis on responsibility is associated—the result of the need to prove one's election—consists of a way of life imbued with rationality. The search for evidence of election in acts of inner-worldly life, specifically in profession, could not occur without a method to allow rational control over human action. For it to generate the best results, it was essential to have predictability, without which one could never know whether their acts would produce positive effects.

The rational control of one's behaviour requires the awareness of how human action will be assessed; that is, it implies predictability of the results of actions and events. The lack of predictability eliminates any possibility of methodical conduct in the exercise of profession.

When one thinks of the optimum exercise of profession as a way of sanctification or of externalizing election, it is not enough to ask about the adequacy of actions towards religious rules, but it is necessary to check whether the action can achieve

[14] The part, therefore, of Catholic morality that essentially distinguishes it from puritan moralism is that the active zeal of the Calvinist is stimulated by the single and unshakable certainty that he is saved by the one and sovereign decree of God, while the Catholic believes in the duty of acting morally to influence the final decree of God. And what distinguishes this asceticism from the medieval one is that, then, the believer sought loyalty to a rigid morality that should not be defiled by secular activities; Luther had fully removed the barriers of the convent; his asceticism, however, maintains the traditional reluctance against the activities of a particular political and professional world. Calvinism, on the contrary, introduced an ascetic ideal within the century (*innerhalb des weltlichen Berufslebens*) and even in the most profane professional activities. It goes even further: it is in the test of the temporal activities that faith is found. If he is a reprobate, man will visibly appear as such in the way he behaves in profane tasks; if he is elected, on the contrary, all his activities will externalize the mark of divine blessings. Biéler (2012), p. 590.

[15] The elimination of magic as a means of salvation was not carried out in Catholic piety with the same consequences it had in puritan religiosity (and, before that, only in Judaism). The Catholic had, at his disposal, the sacramental grace of his Church to compensate for his own insufficiency: the priest was a magician who performed the miracle of transubstantiation and in whose hands the power of the keys was placed. One could turn to him in repentance and penance; he ministered atonement, the hope of grace, and the certainty of forgiveness and, in this way, enabled the release of that enormous tension in which the Calvinist was inescapably and relentlessly bound to live. For the latter, there were no friendly and humane consolations, nor was it possible for him to hope to repair moments of weakness and levity with redoubled goodwill at other times, as Catholics and Lutherans could. The Calvinist God demanded from his followers not isolated good works but a sanctification through works erected in a system. (Not even thinking about the Catholic and authentically human back and forth between sin, repentance, penance, relief and, again, sin, nor thinking about that kind of lifelong balance to be paid off either through temporal penalties or through ecclesiastical grace.) The ethical praxis of ordinary mortals was thus stripped of its lack of overall plan and systematicity and converted into a coherent method of conducting life. It was not by chance that the label "methodists" stuck to those who were the bearers of the last great reawakening of puritan ideals in the eighteenth century, in the same way that was placed on their spiritual ancestors of the seventeenth century, with full equivalence of meaning, the name of "precisists". Weber (2004a, b, c), pp. 106–107.

a result that will please God. Therefore, it is imperative that the rules governing an individual's life be predictable. That is to say, the predictability of law is essential to the appropriate practice of profession, obtaining, in this way, a result that constitutes a sign of election. Without predictability, individuals have no way of knowing whether their methodical action will allow them to achieve the desired results. Religion enters here as a stimulus for the due exercise of a profession and to obtain an optimum result, not, of course, as an indication or sign that this result will be obtained. This means that the values of Protestantism, in the same way that they are intimately related to the "spirit" of capitalism, may equally be associated with the rationality of the law.

2.2 Rationality of Law, Capitalism and Religion

To develop capitalism, it was essential to have a rational and predictable law. Weber, in *A gênese do capitalismo moderno*, after reflecting on the complete irrationality of primitive Chinese law, argues that, with a law of this strain, capitalism cannot operate. What it needs is a calculable law, similar to a machine. Religious-ritualistic and magical aspects must not have any significance.[16] Pointing to this passage from Weber, Jessé Souza[17] notes that formal rational law is perceived by Weber as fundamental to the existence of modern capitalism *because of its calculable nature and its predictability*. It would not be possible to engage in planning or calculation in the long-term, activities that are essential to the existence of a competitive market based on *impersonal* principles, if justice depended on magical assumptions, as in the case of this particular passage, citing the example of Chinese society, or on the discretion of judges who decide according to their own will. Swedberg[18] also observes that Weberian sociology of economics gives special attention to the law, emphasizing that one of the preconditions of rational Western capitalism, according to Weber, "is a rational Law, that is to say, predictable".

There is no doubt that, for Weber, there is an intimate relationship between the rationality of law and capitalism, as well as a clear connection between ascetic Protestantism and capitalism. However, it remains necessary to investigate the possible association between Protestantism and the rationality of law.

Of course, no one ever intended to say that were it not for the values of Calvinism, capitalism would not have developed but that these values contributed to a social behaviour—inner-worldly asceticism—that made up the capitalist "spirit" and, therefore, led to its development. On the other hand, capitalism, to evolve, depended on the rationality and predictability of law.

---

[16] Weber (2006), p. 95.

[17] Souza (2006), p. 95.

[18] Swedberg (2005), p. 155.

However, there is no reason to associate Protestantism only with capitalism when we understand that the rationality of law, which was a precondition for the development of capitalism, suffered no influence from Protestantism. As said before, Protestantism also contributed to a methodical life endowed with rationality. The action of the individual, because it cannot turn itself off from an optimum end or outcome as proof of election, was a rational action, which could not neglect predictability so that life guided by inner-worldly asceticism, a feature of Calvinism, also demanded a rational law marked by predictability. It should be stressed that the interest of Protestants—who made up the frames of the bourgeoisie—in the calculability of law is underscored by Weber.[19]

We do not purport to believe, evidently, that the rationality of law has ascetic Protestantism as a cause, more so a main cause. Remember that not only Weber believed that European law was more rational than systems from other civilizations, but he also argued that this law was shaped according to several features particular to the history of Western law—such as the tradition of Roman law and aspects of medieval law—and was the recipient of an influx of broad and diverse religious, economic and political trends in Western life.[20] Therefore, what must really be made clear is that as the values of Protestantism gave rise to a way of living that is identified as the "spirit" of capitalism, assisting in its development, it is possible to argue that these same values contributed to a rational way of life and to the rationalization of law. In strictly Weberian terms, it can be stated that there is adequate causation between predictable law and a systematic and methodical way of life resulting from inner-worldly asceticism.

It should be noted that if business improvement is a rationally oriented pursuit according to religious values and if, therefore, it is essential to have a rational and predictable law, the relationship between the values of Calvinism and the rationality of law becomes a little more overt. It helps to consider here Weber's typology of rationally determined social action in relation to ends and values. According to Weber,[21] social action, like all action, can be determined (i) rationally by a means-end relationship (*zweckrational*): by forming expectations about the behaviour of exterior objects and other persons and by taking these expectations as conditions or means to achieve one's own rationally pondered and pursued ends, such as success; (ii) rationally by values—value-rational social action (*wertrational*): by a conscious belief in an absolute value—whether it is ethical, aesthetic, religious or interpreted in any other form—inherent to a set behaviour as such, regardless of the outcome; (iii) by affection, especially emotional: social action determined by one's affections or current emotional state; and (iv) by tradition: social action determined by deeply rooted customs.

---

[19] Naturally, it is all up to the interested bourgeois parties to demand an unequivocal, clear right, free of irrational administrative discretion and irrational disturbances by concrete privileges, a right that, first of all, secures the legally binding nature of contracts and that, by virtue of all these qualities, operates in a calculable way. Weber (2004a, b, c), p. 123.

[20] Trubeck (1972), p. 737.

[21] Weber (2004a, b, c), p. 15.

Admittedly, Calvinists, as they led their life, were guided by religious values, even though they were looking for outward signs of their election, i.e. the outcomes that bespoke their salvation. So one can say that Calvinists acted rationally towards an end—obtaining success in the profession or in business—but at the same time acted rationally according to a religious value—the doctrine of predestination. It would even be possible to say that rational action, encompassed in methodical and systematic work, would be determined, at the same time, by an end and a value. Pierucci, in his thesis on the Weberian concept of "disenchantment of the world", affirms that Weber tried to show that, with this coincidence between professional activity and the inner certainty of the salvation of the soul acquired in the act of working rationally, ascetic Protestantism produced an unbreakable and singular unity between rational action towards ends (Zweckrationalität) and rational action relating to values (Wertrationalität) and that, in this, there would have been, in other terms, a historically unprecedented fit between practical-technical rationality and practical-ethical rationality.[22]

However, if it is possible to see here a way of action determined by and end and a value, which fulfils the conditions of practical rationality in its entirety, there is no way not to notice that this action, be it to obtain the end, be it to not digress from the value, cannot do without a rational and predictable law. Undoubtedly, besides the "Protestant" conduct being an undeniably rational action, driven by a religious value and concerned with obtaining an end, this action demanded, to avoid frustration, a law able to guarantee the end or the result. The law certainly does not aim to guarantee the value but rather the end, the attainment of which matters for its concretization. The law operates there as an instrument to rationalize a life guided by religion and targeted at obtaining ends.

José Eduardo Faria, in the preface to the known Anthony Kronman's book on Weber's legal sociology, recalls that Weber demonstrates, through the study of Islam, Judaism and ancient China, how modern history is characterized by the progressive rationalization of all sectors of life, converting efficiency and calculation into ultimate criteria. Rational action that thus ensues, which always establishes relationships between means and ends, could be seen as (i) *practical material action*, which involves choosing available and efficient means to achieve an end; (ii) *material rational action*, founded on values chosen according to personal conviction; and (iii) *formal rational action*, which requires impersonal, abstract and general rules logically sequenced to guide social behaviour.[23] After warning that formal rational action (iii), because it sets standards and generates expectations that they will be observed, is the one that offers more predictability and probability of their occurrence, Faria emphasizes that an emblematic example of formal rationality pointed by Weber is positive law, seen by him as a mechanism to increase the likelihood that certain actions manifest in a certain way, that is, in the way that they were prescribed by codes and statutes. By ensuring respect for property as well as the

[22] Pierucci (2005), p. 205.

[23] Faria (2009).

validity and enforceability of contracts, by providing economic agents with the security they need to invest, and by making changes in its own rules and procedures predictable, positive law works as a "mitigator" of the indeterminacy of social actions as a mechanism to facilitate human interactions and as a reference point for the so-called rules of the game. It is based on this line of reasoning that Weber explains how political thought, legislation, administration of justice and economic practices, in the transition from the medieval to the modern world, free themselves from all fetters expressed by myths, taboos and mysteries, in such a way that the separation between the transcendent God and a world without magic is completed by Protestantism of a Calvinistic nature and by the subsequent advent of modernity and capitalism.[24]

I make reference to José Eduardo Faria's preface to underscore the umbilical relationship between rational action directed to ends and encouraged by values, proper to life marked by ascetic Protestantism, and the rationality of law. The exercise of profession by the Calvinist, an action targeted towards success to prove election and, therefore, equally grounded in values, could not do without *formal rational action*, that is, positive law, the only way to guarantee the expectations placed on the energy expended while working, that is to say, the only way to justify the exercise of a profession itself as a mechanism to attest the predetermination of election.

In short, inner-worldly asceticism, or more specifically the performance of work as a means of proof of salvation, is nothing more than a clear expression of the "disenchantment with the world", which arose from the breakup with the magic elements of the saving sacraments, an asceticism characterized by rational action, driven by values and directed at ends. Exactly because of this, asceticism could not do without a mechanism—the law—which, with clarity and logic, was able to guarantee the result of energy and value invested in the acts of life.

2.3 Rationality of Law and Predictability

Another point that matters here concerns the meaning, in Weber's view, of the rationality of law and if there is a distinction between formal rationality of law and predictability. Weber points out four ideal types of law: (i) formally irrational law, (ii) substantially irrational law, (iii) substantially rational law and (iv) formally rational law.

Although what is really important in this context is to examine what Weber meant by formally rational law,[25] it is worth remembering that the writings on Weber's theory warn us that these ideal types of law correspond, though not accurately, to the four stages of the historical development of the law examined in

[24] Id.

[25] Swedberg (2005).

Weber's work.[26] The *formally irrational law*, uncontrolled by intellect, averse to general standards and insensitive to the claims of the parties, is the law from the time when decisions were derived from revelations made by an oracle.[27] In *substantially irrational law*, decisions operate through criteria based on practical and ethical considerations in each case.[28] Kadi justice exemplifies materially irrational law. Weber understood Kadi justice as a wider concept than the justice administered by the local Muslim judge. In his view, such a concept represented the idea of judgment made in accordance with the sense of fairness of the judge himself, without any consideration of rules.[29] In *substantially rational law*, decisions operate through laws or criteria, but the system of law, by being anchored on external thought, is dependent on the possibility of understanding the principles that guide the thought that sustains it.[30] Weber alludes, here, to Islamic and Chinese laws. Theocratic power and patrimonial power imposed a systematic form of law influenced by elements that belong, for example, to religion and political ideology. Although these systems have relations with fixed principles, they refuse to recognize any limit to law, and their goal is the realization of ethical, religious or political ideals, which implies the material rationalization of law. Or rather, adherence to fixed principles characterizes the system as rational—unlike the first two—but the idea of achieving religious, ethical and political values makes one suppose a substantive rationalization of law, not a formal one. The fourth type of law, which is placed on a whole other standard compared to the previous ones, is *formally rational law*. It is legislated modern law.[31] Civil codes, which were derived from Roman law and grounded in the teachings of the Pandectists, are prime examples of formally rational law.[32]

But is it the category of formally rational law that truly matters here? To try to understand what is formally rational law for Weber, we need to bear in mind that, for him, only systems developed from Roman law and shaped by Pandectist jurisprudence are able to reflect, on a significant degree, behaviours and methods of a formal and rational nature.[33] As Anthony Kronman ponders, the high degree of formal rationality of these codes is explained by the fact that they are based on the logical interpretation of meaning and possess a highly systematic nature, thus adhering

[26] The creation and enforcement of law can be rational or irrational. They are formally irrational when, to regulate the creation of law and the problems in its enforcement, methods that cannot be rationally controlled are deployed—for example, consulting oracles and their surrogates. Weber (2004a, b, c), p. 12.

[27] Swedberg (2005), p. 166.

[28] Trubeck (1972), p. 748. In Weber's words, law will be materially irrational to the extent that the decision is determined by completely concrete assessments of each case, whether they are of an emotional, political or ethical nature, instead of being determined by general rules. See Weber (2004a, b, c), p. 13.

[29] Swedberg (2005), p. 170.

[30] Trubeck (1972), p. 748.

[31] Swedberg (2005), pp. 166–167.

[32] See Wieacker (1980), p. 348.

[33] Kronman (2009), pp. 127–128.

to the postulates developed by Weber: (i) that each concrete legal decision be the "application" of an abstract legal proposition to a concrete "factual situation"; (ii) that it should be possible, in any case, to derive the decision from abstract legal propositions by means of legal logic; (iii) that law must be, real or virtually, a system of legal propositions with "no gaps" or should at least be treated as a system without gaps; (iv) that everything that cannot be "construed" rationally in legal terms is also legally irrelevant; (v) that all social action of human beings must always be seen as an "application" or "execution" of legal propositions or an "offence" to them, considering that the "no gaps" principle of the legal system must result in a "legal order" encompassing all social behaviour.[34]

Interestingly, Weber noted that the abandonment of oracular justice—in which humans will have no relevance—and the prevalence of a formally rational law brought with it the need to justify the decision, from which predictability arises. As Kronman writes, if people who solve conflicts can claim that they speak in the name of God or of a transcendent power, there may be little pressure on them to state the reasons for their decisions because they themselves are an oracle. However, when cases are solved by a man and not by oracular powers, there is a great practical need for justification. This means that admitting personal responsibility for the decision not only introduced the need for justification but rather also made it possible.[35]

The "disenchantment of law"—which cannot be mistaken with the category of "disenchantment of the world",[36] in the sense that it means only the passage of power to judge from the divine or that is transcendental to men—is of particular importance when the law becomes formally rational. Therein arises the need for a rational demonstration of the decision and, with it, a kind of predictability graced with meaning.[37]

But the idea of predictability, as asserted by Weber, is much broader and can only be understood from the perception of what registers as a legal system or, more precisely from the concepts that, according to him, sustain it, namely the concepts of scope and organizational clarity. As Kronman explains, a legal system is comprehensive only if there is, in principle, no social actions beyond its reach and if it contains no gaps or omissions, and it has organizational clarity if the principles underpinning it are sharply clear and applied self-consciously.[38] This means that, for Weber, the more comprehensive and organizationally clear a legal system is, the more predictable will be the consequences of social actions taken under its guard.

This indicates, therefore, that the idea of predictability, in Weber's view, is not disconnected from the idea of a legal system and, after all, is a largely relative notion, in that it can vary according to the comprehensiveness or clarity of the legal system. Aware of this, Kronman emphasizes that, as English common law shows, a

---

[34] Id., pp. 120–121.

[35] Ibidem, p. 120.

[36] See Pierucci (2005).

[37] Kronman (2009), p. 129.

[38] Id., pp. 137–138.

certain predictability—perhaps even a significant degree of it—can be achieved without building a true legal system. However, the maximum predictability can be achieved only when the rules of the legal order have been organized in a comprehensive and clear way in conceptual terms; however great its predictability is, it is always possible to make a legal system more predictable through its systematization.[39]

There is no identity between the formal rationality of law and predictability as predictability is a consequence of a legal system despite its greater or lesser rationality. Predictability is the goal of a system with comprehensiveness and organizational clarity, but it can stem from a less rational system or even from formally irrational law, such as what Weber considered the primitive English common law. Remember that, according to him, in common law, the degree of legal rationality is significantly lower and of a distinct kind than that of the systems of continental Europe.[40]

One arrives, thus, to the following point: given that England is the birthplace of capitalism and a place where Calvinism was incisively projected, how can Weber's conclusion be explained that English common law is a formally irrational system or that it is unfurnished with the same degree of rationality of European continental law? Had Weber misread the relationship between religion and capitalism? Is there, in Weber's rationale, a poor grasp of the English common law or the history of England? Or, to put it simply, does the system of mandatory precedent have nothing to do with the formal rationality of law?

2.4 The So-Called Problem of England

The argument that Weber's work has a contradiction, or a misunderstanding, arose primarily from an essay by David Trubeck, titled *Max Weber on Law and the Rise of Capitalism*, published in 1972 in the Wisconsin Law Review. In this essay, Trubeck refers to a working paper written by one of his students, Jerold Guben, called *"The England Problem" and the Theory of Economic Development*, presented to Yale Law School's Program in Law and Modernization.

Trubeck claims that Weber equates legal rationality with predictability (or calculability) and believes that the latter is not present in common law, so that England would be an exception to the theory that there is a relationship between capitalism and calculability or an exception to the idea that formal rationality and calculability

[39] Ibidem, p. 138.

[40] Weber (2004a, b, c), p. 150.

necessarily go together.[41] Trubeck cautioned that some observers[42] had said that England developed a system of rational law even before the rise of capitalism and that the great defect of Weber's analysis was on the mistaken distinction he made between English common law and European continental law.[43]

The "problem of England" was also the subject of an analysis by Swedberg.[44] The Swedish sociologist argues that Trubeck misses in stating that, in Weber's work, there is a necessary identity between predictability and a high degree of logical formalism or formal rationality. He notes that Weber makes clear that bourgeois groups demanded predictability from the legal system and that it is fully compatible with a low degree of formal rationality. He also recalls that according to Weber, English common law, although not equipped with formal rationality, is predictable.

---

[41] Trubeck (1972), p. 748: "If these contrasting positions indicate that Weber had no clear image of English history in mind, they also reflect his concern with the issue of legal calculability and his tendency to equate it with one mode of legal thought-a mode of thought which clearly was not well developed in England. His constant temptation was to maintain the key importance of calculability, and deal with England either as an exception to the theory that legal calculability and capitalism are related, or as an exception to the idea that logically formal rationality and calculability necessarily go together".

[42] Notwithstanding, on a footnote, he cites only his student Jerold Guben's work, *"The England Problem" and the Theory of Economic Development.*

[43] Trubeck (1972), p. 748: "some observers have argued that England did develop a truly 'rational' legal system before the rise of capitalism, and that the major flaw in Weber's analysis was the false distinction he drew between English and continental law".

[44] Sally Ewing, in the essay *Formal Justice and the Spirit of Capitalism: Max Weber's Sociology of Law*, published in the *Law and Society Review*, rejects the idea that Weber had defended that a high degree of legal rationality would be essential for the development of capitalism, showing that, in fact, Weber admitted that, for the development of capitalism, it would be enough to have a law capable of facilitating commercial transactions and guaranteeing predictability: "For Weber, the 'legal order' that was relevant to the rise of capitalism was not a particular type of legal thought but a social order in which law facilitated capitalist transactions by contributing to the predictability of social action. [...] Thus, according to Weber, the legal order that was essential to the growth of capitalism was a contractual one that limited patriarchal discretion and protected its subjects' rights to establish contractual relations and to mobilize the coercive apparatus to enforce those contracts. By thus protecting and enforcing a set of social relations, law became explicitly relevant to economics. It was, in other words, 'a complex of actual determinants of human conduct'. It made no particular difference whether those relations were defined by a logically formal system or a more informal common law system. To the extent that each system defended the freedom of contract and protected guaranteed rights, the capitalist economic order could thrive. This brings us back to the question about the relationship between types of legal thought and the rise of capitalism. If one concentrates, as Rheinstein did, on legal thought itself, then according to Weber's ideal types common law would be considered 'substantively irrational', while civil law would be classified as 'logically formally rational' (Weber 1954, p. xiii). But if one is concerned not with legal thought but with empirical validity, then Weber quite clearly set out the historical conditions that in England gave birth to a legal system that was particularly well suited to the demands of the bourgeoisie for guaranteed rights and formal justice, the characteristics that distinguish a bourgeois, or liberal, legal system from all those that preceded it. In this sense the common law system, with its 'formal rational administration of justice' (Weber 1978: vol. 2, p. 813) and in spite of all its juridical irrationality, was certainly a formal, rational legal system in the sociological sense of the term." Ewing (1987), pp. 498–499.

He argues further that Trubeck's formulation of the problem of England implies an overly narrow view of the relationship between capitalism and law since for rational capitalism to exist, it is not enough to have predictability and a high degree of formal rationality, but it is also necessary to have sophisticated legal rules about a large number of advanced economic institutions, especially economic and business contracts, something that is recognized by Weber.

Swedberg's main argument is that Trubeck had made a mistake in finding Weber a necessary identity between predictability and a high degree of formal legal rationality. This mistake, in fact, was anticipated by the reasons given in the previous section, when it clarified that predictability is the goal of a system with comprehensiveness and organizational clarity, but it can stem from a less rational law or even from a formally irrational law. As stated by Anthony Kronman, the establishment of an efficient capitalist mode of production does not presuppose the maximum level of predictability attainable through the formal rationalization of law, so there is no contradiction between Weber's claim on the lesser rationalization of English law and the capitalist development in England.[45]

Undoubtedly, not only is it possible to extract from Weber's arguments the view that English common law, although not supplied with the same degree of rationality as continental European law, was predictable,[46] but it is also possible to find Weber's passages that clearly assert it—as the one remembered by Swedberg.

To understand the reason why Weber did not see formal legal rationality in early English law, it is necessary to observe that common law, because it was not concerned with abstraction, did not stimulate the formulation of general principles.[47] There was no way to produce "general concepts", given that concrete rules arose from cases and were differentiated according to external criteria. Rules of this sort, though numerous, cannot claim to have "comprehensiveness", which, as seen, along with organizational clarity, defined the Weberian ideal of a legal system.[48]

---

[45] In light of this interpretation, the apparent tension between Weber's claim that "formally rational law and administration" are prerequisites to achieve the highest possible degree of predictability in economic action and his claim that the capitalist enterprise developed in England in spite of the irrationality of common law simply disappears: a contradiction only exists if we compare the maximum degree of legal predictability that can be reached through formal rationalization with the minimum degree required for an initial establishment of an effective capitalist production system. Kronman (2009), p. 189.

[46] Hubert Treiber, when examining the "problem of England", points out that "the peculiar nature of modern capitalism, especially its technical and economic substructure, requires that success be calculable, and law figures as one means to assure this. However—and this is decisive to the argument—in England and Germany the chances that law and adjudication would be rendered calculable depended on different premises. [...] Despite the rationalization differential between England and Germany with respect to the formal qualities of law, legal proceedings were predictable in both places due to the predictability of the judges, though this may have been assured in different ways." Treiber (1985), pp. 841–842.

[47] Remember that part of the English doctrine of the late eighteenth century and early nineteenth century, unhappy with the lack of rationality and predictability of common law, joined the plea for written law. See Bentham (1843) and Austin (1911).

[48] Kronman (2009), p. 139.

But this did not mean that English common law, for Weber, was devoid of any degree of predictability. Weber admits that predictability can be achieved not only through a system with general principles and that is able, because of this, to achieve the comprehensiveness of all imaginable situations. Kronman clearly demonstrates, alluding to Weber's discussion, that even if a legal system lacks comprehensiveness and organizational clarity, a sufficiently high degree of predictability can be reached if those responsible for administering the rules understand and respect the contractual agreements and understandings based on customary law that defines most commercial transactions.[49]

Weber also considers *stare decisis* (the system of mandatory precedent) an element of importance for achieving predictability.[50] This, indeed, is expressly recognized by Kronman when he points to the contrast that Weber draws between oracle-based law and judicial decisions in common law, which, by requiring justification, according to Weber, tends to make the legal system more predictable. Actually, unless we suppose that the formation of precedents (which refers to the reasons for the decision) and the rule of *stare decisis* significantly increase the predictability of legal outcomes, it is difficult to explain the positive contribution made by the English legal system to the development of a rational, capitalist economy based on market exchange in England, a form of economic organization that, according to Weber, requires a predictable application of a stable set of legal rules.[51]

Given that reasoning is a requirement for the rationality of a system of precedent, it is obvious that a contribution to predictability and, consequently, to the development of capitalism was found in *stare decisis*, i.e. in the justified and rational belief that the delivery of justice would not leave entrepreneurs helpless. We should note that Kronman not only says that *stare decisis* significantly contributed to predictability, but he also argues that without *stare decisis*, it would be difficult to explain the positive contribution made by common law to the development of capitalism.

Thus, it is correct to say that *stare decisis* was an important element in balancing out the absence of systematicity in common law, having contributed significantly to its predictability and thereby mitigating the lack of formal legal rationality of English law under Weberian terms.

---

[49] Id., pp. 187–188.

[50] And there are also escape valves for legal formalism. In private law, common law and equity are, without a doubt, largely "formalistic" in practical application due to their connection to precedents. It is noteworthy that in this context, the term "formalism" is synonymous with predictability. Weber (2004a, b, c), p. 150.

[51] Ibidem, p. 135.

2.5 Summary of Ideas

Calvinist values brought about a rational behaviour that contributed to the development of capitalism and called for a rational and predictable law. This means that the values and culture of a people can and should be related to the rationality of law and the administration of justice. This first idea is very important because I intend to establish later a relationship between Brazilian culture, the irrational administration of justice and the absence of a system of precedents.

On the other hand, Weber did not identify formal legal rationality with predictability but, instead, saw on *stare decisis* a mechanism capable of providing predictability in a formally irrational law, which means that, although common law does not hold the same kind of rationality as traditional European continental law, it was able to secure, because of a system of binding precedents, a degree of predictability that allowed the flourishing of capitalism.

Trubeck's view[52] that Weber's argument was inconsistent because he admitted that England, the cradle of capitalism, had a formally irrational law, does not withstand the fact that Weber never actually took formal legal rationality as predictability and, also, that he saw on *stare decisis* an efficient way of guaranteeing it, which would have allowed the development of capitalism even in a system devoid of formal rationality.

It is clear that Weber, when comparing common law with European continental law, acknowledged the formal rationality of the latter because of its nature at that historical moment. We ought to remember that he was particularly facing scientific positivism, German conceptualism, interpretive cognitivism and logicism in adjudication when he was reaching that conclusion. This means that, as will be shown in the following chapters, the evolution of the interpretation theory, the impact of constitutionalism and the transformation of the very concept of law created a new legal rationality in civil law, which therefore may require and coexist with a system of binding precedents.

Moreover, common law, by not having the same formal rationality of legislated law, adopted *stare decisis* to counterbalance its lack of rationality and predictability. To reaffirm that common law is not the same as *stare decisis* is obviously something that need not be evidenced by the work of Weber.[53] But the opportunity Weber offers to demonstrate that *stare decisis* is an instrument for achieving predictability in a law perceived as less rational than that of a time of scientific positivism has great relevance to the point of indispensability of a system of precedents in contemporary Brazilian law, among other systems, wherein it became quite common to decide like cases differently without giving any importance to predictability, an essential moral value for the development of men and a necessary requisite for economic rationality.

---

[52] Trubeck (1972), p. 748.

[53] Simpson (1973), p. 77: "To a historian at least any identification between the *common law* system and the doctrine of precedent, any attempt to explain the nature of the *common law* in terms of *stare decisis*, is bound to seem unsatisfactory, for the elaboration of rules and principles governing the use of precedents and their status as authorities is relatively modern, and the idea that there could be binding precedents more recent still. The *common law* had been in existence for centuries before anybody was very excited about these matters, and yet it functioned as a system of law without such props as the concept of the *ratio decidendi*, and functioned well enough."

References

Austin J (1911) Lectures on jurisprudence, or the philosophy of positive law, vol 2, 5th edn. John Murray

Bentham J (1843) Truth versus Ashhurst; or law as it is, contrasted with what it is said to be. The works of Jeremy Bentham, vol 5. William Tait

Biéler A (2012) O pensamento econômico e social de Calvino. Editora Cultura Cristã

Ewing S (1987) Formal justice and the spirit of capitalism: Max Weber's sociology of law. Law Soc Rev 21:487–512

Faria JF (2009) Prefácio em "Max Weber", de Anthony Kronman. Elsevier

Kronman A (2009) Max Weber. Elsevier

Pierucci AF (2005) O desencantamento do mundo – Todos os passos do conceito em Max Weber. Editora 34

Simpson AWB (1973) The common law and legal theory. Oxford essays in jurisprudence. Clarendon Press

Souza J (2006) Comentários à obra "A gênese do capitalismo moderno", de Max Weber. Ática

Swedberg R (2005) Max Weber e a ideia de sociologia econômica. Ed. UFRJ

Treiber H (1985) 'Elective affinities' between Weber's sociology of religion and sociology of law. Theory Soc 14:809–861

Trubeck DM (1972) Max Weber on law and the rise of capitalism. Wis Law Rev 3:720–753

Weber M (2004a) A ética protestante e o "espírito" do capitalismo. Companhia das Letras

Weber M (2004b) Economia e Sociedade, vol 1. Editora UnB

Weber M (2004c) Economia e sociedade, vol 2. Editora UnB

Weber M (2006) A gênese do capitalismo moderno. Ática

Wieacker F (1980) História do Direito Privado moderno (Privatrechtsgeschichte der Neuzeit unter besonderer Berücksichtigung der deutschen Entwicklung). Tradução de Antônio Manuel Hespanha. Fundação Calouste Gulbenkian

Chapter 3
The Transformation of Civil Law

Contents

This chapter aims to briefly demonstrate the changes that civil law has experienced due to the recent trends in constitutionalism and in legal interpretation. It concludes, after going through these trends, that in civil law systems, the concepts of law and jurisdiction have undergone profound transformation.

3.1 Systematicity, Comprehensiveness and Predictability in Civil Law Tradition

In scientific positivism—the basis of German Pandectism—law is derived from concepts and general principles developed by legal science. Rules are logically inferred from the system—that is, from its principles and general concepts—without incorporating elements from non-legal orders. Issues of moral, religious, political or economic nature, or rather matters that cannot be directly derived from the legal system itself, cannot be taken into account.[1]

The legal system is autonomous and independent from social reality, and owes its consistency to the institutions and rules that give it its singular content. Cases can be solved by a mere logical operation of subsumption of the real and concrete situation to a hypothetical valuation contained in a general doctrinal principle and

[1] Wieacker (1980), p. 431. See also Larenz (2012), p. 9 et seq; Chiassoni (2009), p. 177 et seq.

L. G. Marinoni, *Culture and Predictability of Law*, SpringerBriefs in Law,
https://doi.org/10.1007/978-3-031-87161-0_3

implicit on scientific concepts. In them, permanently valid principles about the correction of law are present, so that the logical application of the concept and the principle is enough to reach a correct or fair decision.[2]

The system is not only *closed*—autonomous and consistent—but it also enjoys *completeness*. Based on concepts and logical connections, it will always be possible to remedy deficiencies of law through what became known as "creative construction". Legal and scientific concepts are developed and structured specifically to enable the logical subsumption of concrete situations, eliminating gaps in positive law.

It is important to understand that the pursuit of wholeness through conceptualization had a clear objective of ensuring predictability and certainty in law enforcement. If the resolution of cases depends solely on logical reasoning guided by concepts and legal-scientific principles, without being based on moral standards, religious norms etc., the ideal of achieving predictability and certainty of law becomes feasible without the need to use criteria outside of legal concepts or other means, such as a system of mandatory precedents. That—it should be stressed from the outset—is clearly incompatible with a system of decisions that cannot stay detached from issues of a moral, economic or political nature, wherein the particularities of the conflict are essential to delivering justice in the case.[3]

That said, scientific positivism is not the same as legalistic positivism. The first is based on concepts and general principles of a scientific nature, while the latter is premised on the idea that law exists only in legislation.[4] The difference becomes clearer as we recall that German legal science, especially in the first half of the nineteenth century, was concerned with elaborating a dogmatic doctrine capable of addressing the absence of a common code of private law in all of Germany. From the second half of the nineteenth century, however, several German States adopted codes, and the liberal movement for unification imposed, even after its political defeat, the continuation of the codification of common law throughout Germany.[5] That is why in place of scientific positivism, the field became open to legalistic positivism. According to Franz Wieacker, this was a victory, albeit not fully realized and recognized by social consciousness, of a political nation over a cultural nation.[6]

Leaving aside the history of German law, it is worth remembering that, unlike what happened in England, the Parliamentary Assembly of French law, while

[2] Wieacker (1980), p. 430 et seq.

[3] In truth, as Franz Wieacker has argued, the original function as well of scientific positivism, from the point of view of legal politics, is today distorted to the point of having become unrecognizable, due to the social and political changes of the last hundred years and the ideological criticism that stemmed from these changes. An application of law that excludes, in principle, 'political, social or economic considerations' can no longer be seen as correct in a time of ideological and social struggles. Wieacker (1980), p. 501.

[4] See Hespanha (2012), p. 413 et seq.

[5] Wieacker (1980), pp. 524–525.

[6] It means that for the first time after its reception the state creation of law in Germany has become independent of erudite doctrine (id., p. 525).

defeating the monarch, monopolized power through the principle of legality.[7] Also derived from this is the impossibility of confusing the English rule of law with the principle of legality.[8] If—as Carl Schmitt says—in the idealization of the liberal State of law the bourgeoisie adopted a concept of law that rested on an old European tradition—a heritage of Greek philosophy, which came to the modern age through scholasticism—according to which statutes are not the will of one man or many men but are a general-rational thing (not *voluntas* but *ratio*),[9] in the historical process of affirmation of the bourgeoisie, this notion of law gave way to its opposite, a concept of law championed by representatives of State absolutism, according to which, in the classical formula coined by Hobbes—*auctoritas, non veritas facit legem*—the law is will, valid not due to logical and moral qualities but precisely as an order.

The principle of legality eventually became a criterion for identifying law. Law would exist only in legal norms, whose validity depends not on their correspondence with justice but on having been made by an authority endowed with legislative powers. From this, Ferrajoli qualifies the principle of legality as a meta-rule for the recognition of existing standards, adding that according to this principle, a legal rule exists and is valid only according to how it was produced. The legality of the rule does not depend on its fairness, and what matters only is whether it was made by a competent authority and according to a regular procedure.[10]

During this liberal State of law, parliaments of continental Europe secured to themselves political power based on the principle of legality. Given the hegemony of parliament, the executive and the judiciary took obvious positions of subordination. The executive could act only if authorized by law and within its exact boundaries, and the judiciary could only apply it, without even having the capacity to interpret it. The legislature thus took a clear position of superiority. The principle of legality was closely linked to the principle of freedom, a value pursued by the liberal State, drawing on the ideas that the executive could only do what the law authorized and that citizens could do everything that the law did not forbid. Equality, which disregarded the real circumstances of people, was seen as a guarantee of freedom, i.e. of the non-discrimination of social positions, regardless of whether there were glaring concrete distinctions among them. The liberal State was concerned with defending the citizens against any aggression of State authority and not with their

---

[7] Gustavo Zagrebelsky (2003). On the importance of constitutional history or, rather, of critical history to best understand contemporary constitutional law, see Zagrebelsky (2005).

[8] Dicey characterizes the *rule of law* by three elements: the absence of arbitrary power, equality before the law and, lastly, the fact that constitutional general principles are the results the of a common law, i.e. they are revealed in the way through which courts enforce individual rights. Dicey (1959), pp. 202–203. See Rosenfeld (2001), p. 1307.

[9] *Schmitt (*1982*), p. 150.*

[10] Ferrajoli (2001), p. 52.

various social needs.[11] The impossibility of the State interfering in society,[12] to protect disadvantaged social positions, was a natural consequence of the assumption that to preserve freedom for all, it was necessary not to discriminate against anyone, as any differential treatment was seen as violating equality—logically understood here in its formal dimension only.[13]

The empire of the law, as an instrument in the service of bourgeois freedom, was defined in contrast to the idea of the empire of men. Empire of the law means, above all, that the legislator himself is bound by the laws he enacts. Binding the legislature to the law is only possible, however, to the extent that the law is a rule with specific properties.[14] These are summarized in the concept of general and abstract rules. In order not to violate freedom and equality, the law must retain the characteristics of generality and abstraction. The rule cannot be directed at someone specifically or be made for a particular hypothesis. Generality was thought of as guaranteeing the impartiality of power towards citizens—who, by being "equal" should be treated without discrimination—and abstraction as a guarantee of the stability—in the long term—of the legal system.[15]

To develop society based on freedom, a predictable law or the so-called "certainty of law" was sought. An abstract and general law was favoured that could accommodate any future situation and eliminate the possibility of judges considering the specific circumstances of conflicts when making decisions. Otherwise, the predictability and certainty of law would be compromised, despite the fact that they are indispensable to preserving freedom. It is possible to understand, in this dimension, why Montesquieu noted that if trials were private opinions of judges, people would live in a society without precisely knowing the commitments they are making within it.[16] There is no doubt that this insight by Montesquieu reveals a political ideology linked to the idea that political freedom, seen as an individual's psychological safety, is fulfilled by the principle of "certainty of law".[17]

---

[11] This model is based on the premise that the constitution of a democratic State must primarily repel the dangers that may arise in the space between the State and citizens, therefore in the relations between the administrative apparatus that holds the monopoly of power and private, unarmed, people. On the other hand, horizontal relationships between private persons, especially intersubjective relationships, have no bearing in the liberal scheme of the division of power. Habermas (1997), p. 305.

[12] Schmitt defines classical liberalism's rule of law as a State that respects unconditionally the current objective law and the subjective rights that exist, and he warns that such a conception tends to legitimize and eternalize the current *status quo*. Schmitt (1982), p. 150.

[13] Exemplary, in this sense, is the decision of the Supreme Court of the United States in *Adkins v. Children's Hospital*, 261 U.S. 525 (1923), which struck down a statute that established a minimum wage for women and children. See Sunstein (1993), p. 145.

[14] Schmitt (1982), p. 150.

[15] Zagrebelsky (1992), pp. 32–33. See Corwin (1910), p. 102.

[16] Montesquieu (1973), p. 158.

[17] Tarello (1976), p. 294. See Hazard Jr. (1984–1985), pp. 646–647.

Positivism is characterized by systematicity and completeness and has as its goals legal certainty and predictability. We should note that here lie the requirements of comprehensiveness and organizational clarity claimed by Weber to be necessary for achieving formal legal rationality. The idea of legislative supremacy proposed that the law and statutes should be so clear and complete that they could only yield a single interpretation, one that is unquestionably correct.[18] Rules, seen as elements that form a coherent legal oeuvre that is imbued with clarity, allow judges to extract the principles underpinning them in order to identify, when faced with a gap, the rule necessary to resolve the case in a manner that is consistent with the system and that relates systematicity not only to completeness but also to predictability.[19]

3.2 The Impact of Constitutionalism

The notion of a general, abstract rule, coherent and a product of the homogeneous will of parliament, typical of the law of the French Revolution, did not survive historical developments. People suffered through legislative majorities creating selfish and discriminatory laws. Hence, it became necessary to rescue the substance of the law and to find the tools that could protect the values of justice denied by legislation. This "substance" and these "values" infiltrated constitutions, which ceased to be flexible to become rigid, in the sense of being unmodifiable by ordinary legislation. Constitutions began to have full normative efficacy, causing statutes to lose their position of supremacy.[20]

Legislation became subject to limitation and shaping by principles and constitutional rules, meaning it ceased to have merely formal legitimacy but instead was substantially tied to the rights enshrined in the constitution. If it was possible to say before that fundamental rights were written around statutes, it would now be more accurate to state that laws themselves must be in accordance with fundamental rights.[21] The very principle of legality takes on another meaning, leaving behind its strictly formal nature to acquire a substantial one. The principle of legality binds itself to the content of the rule, or rather, to the conformation of the rule with fundamental rights.

---

[18] Cappelletti (2001), p. 271.

[19] Until the first decades of the twentieth century, the liberal paradigm of law expressed a widespread consensus among legal experts, thus preparing a context of unquestioned maxims of interpretation for the application of the law. This circumstance explains why many thought the law could be applied on its own time, without resorting to principles in need of interpretation or to dubious 'key-concepts'. Habermas (1997), p. 313. In the liberal age—the age that ends in 1914 amidst the splendor of the Great War—the normative system gravitates completely around the Civil Code. The 1865 Civil Code contains general principles, which guide the regulation of particular institutions or subjects and that, ultimately, serve to fill the gaps in the legal system. Irti (1999), p. 133. See also Zagrebelsky (1992), p. 53.

[20] Pierlingieri (1991) and Häberle (1972).

[21] Alexy (2001) and Scheuner (1971).

The mutation of the principle of legality led Ferrajoli to talk about a second revolution, opposed to the one tied to the old principle of legality, which had caused, by asserting the omnipotence of the legislature, a paradigmatic shift from the law before that of the legislative State. This second revolution also led to a paradigmatic shift, replacing the principle of formal legality with the principle of substantive legality.[22] At first sight, one could deny any paradigm shift, preferring to see in this change a mere reaffirmation of the supremacy of the law, arguing that it is simply the full completion of the subjection of the State to the law, consistent in the subordination of legislation itself to a "higher law". However, this reading is an unwarranted reductionism of what it means to subject the law to the constitution, or a misunderstanding of the tensions that led to the transformation of the very notion of law. In fact, the subordination of the law to the constitution cannot be understood as a mere "continuation" of the principles of the legislative State because it means a "transformation" that affects the very concepts of law and adjudication.[23]

There is no doubt that civil law has undergone a process that transformed the concepts of law and adjudication. If the law can no longer be found solely in legislation because it now depends on the constitution, adjudication now has the task of reviewing the validity of legislation according to fundamental rights. Jurisdictions of continental Europe succumbed to the need to review statutes, although this role was initially reserved for entities that, at first, were not conceived to be adjudicative precisely in homage to the principle that judges could not interfere in the legislative task.

The activity of submitting the law to the constitution was not limited to striking down an unconstitutional laws, but, in light of the theoretical dissociation between legal text and legal norm, also allowed the preservation of the law by casting aside unconstitutional interpretations and declaring a constitutional result based on the interpretation of the law. Remember that when the Italian Constitutional Court effectively began operating—after a delay of almost 10 years due to suspicions regarding judicial review—one of the first problems it had to solve was identifying the object of constitutional review of legislation. The Constitutional Court concluded that it was not the text of the statute, but the norm (the result-interpretation) that is expressed by it. This structural separation between text and norm had two very significant advantages: (i) it allowed the declaration of unconstitutionality of a statute or of an interpretation while preserving the legal text or the statute, and (ii) it favoured the practice of interpretating the meaning of legal texts in best agreement with the constitution.[24]

In Brazil, the impact of constitutionalism was greater, given that any judge, based on the theoretical proposition that the validity of the law should be read under fundamental rights, acquired the power to give meaning to those fundamental rights.

---

[22] Ferrajoli (2001), p. 53.

[23] Irti (2005).

[24] Ascarelli (1957), Crisafulli (1964), Tarello (1966, 1980), Guastini (1989, 2011), Chiassoni (2007, 2011).

Needless to say, the task of giving meaning to a fundamental right is something that is beyond the judicial reasoning framed by classical positivism—cognitive interpretation of a pre-existing standard exclusively given by the legislature and logical application of the rule—because it reveals the need to consider factors that must be observed and understood through other points of view, such as morality and economics. Therefore, the true meaning of the transformation of the judicial function is that, by subjecting laws to fundamental rights, judges became required to consider, in addition to the duty of reasoning according to principles that project inaccurate shapes, questions of moral, political and economic nature that are written in the open texture of constitutional provisions, which greatly amplifies the latitude of judicial authority to express the meaning of law and to solve cases. Obviously, this led to the collapse of the belief that the judge could decide by mere logical reasoning, subsuming the concrete situations to abstract hypotheses contained in the legal system. This therefore eliminated claim of legal certainty and predictability of the positivist theory of the late nineteenth and early twentieth centuries' civil law, branded by the ideas of systematicity and comprehensiveness.

Although judicial decisions may not avoid interpreting the meaning of fundamental rights and the consideration of those elements that, although not defined by legal rules, are essential to their understanding, there is no rationality in giving each and every judge the power to develop the meaning of a fundamental right and, despite this, leave them unbound by supreme courts' final word on the same questions. The reason for this is that, in any rational judicial system, it is up to top courts the definition of the meaning of rights, particularly fundamental ones, which by logic makes it incomprehensible the possibility of a judge or an ordinary court giving a particular constitutional provision a different meaning than that which has been assigned by the supreme court.

Indeed, a system that admits a diffuse control of constitutionality cannot let judges and ordinary courts disregard the constitutional precedents of its supreme court. Otherwise, there will be internal incoherence, irrationality and a stimulus to chaos. In fact, Brazilian law, by allowing diffuse judicial review—proper to American law—became incompatible with its own legal practice, by which ordinary courts do not bow to the authority of constitutional precedents.

This, in effect, deserves a sociological analysis, because the explanation for disregarding constitutional precedents—something that, after all, matter to many social groups—should be sought in the factors that stimulated and still stimulate inconsistency and irrationality.

Since the meaning of a fundamental right cannot vary according to the judge or the court, it seems certain that the model of diffuse judicial review is incompatible with a system that ignores something similar to *stare decisis*. Remember that the possibility of diffuse review under civil law was discussed by Mauro Cappelletti. According to him, the introduction of the American method of judicial review into civil law led to the following consequence: a law could be denied enforceability by some judges and courts that found it unconstitutional but, at the same time, could be enforced by other judges and courts that deemed it constitutional, which creates serious legal uncertainty and conflict within the judiciary.[25] This circumstance, of impressive obviousness, has long been ignored in Brazil, certainly for some unspeakable reason that prefers to bet on the irrationality of the legal system.

3.3 Judicial Decision in the Case of Insufficient Legal Protection of a Fundamental Right

After World War II, probably due to the cultural projection of the United States, it became frequent in civil law systems to talk about *judge made law*, which led to the development of theories that gave the judge, based on the maxims of experience and general principles, the exercise of functions that went beyond positive law.[26] There is no doubt this creative approach picked up steam with the recognition of the normative force of constitutional norms, given their significance in the performance of adjudication in the event of insufficient legislative protection of fundamental rights.

In Brazil, there are several class actions whose claimants, when they request the protection of a particular diffuse or collective right, argue the absence of statutory protection of that fundamental right. Also common are individual lawsuits which, based on a fundamental right being *normatively unprotected*, demand a factual provision to be provided by the State.

We ought to remember that the protection of fundamental rights may depend on imperative or prohibitive rules. For instance, to protect environmental and consumer rights, a rule may impose positive or negative action upon people and organizations, such as forcing someone to adopt (positive rule) technology to reduce the emission of gases and pollutants or to not market (negative rule) products containing certain substances. Furthermore, there is also the case where State action, though factual in nature, relies on the previous enactment of a legal rule. This is what happens, for example, in litigation over medication freely distributed by the State, in which individual parties request the State to provide medicines not foreseen in the legislation governing this public policy.

Canaris warns that fundamental rights function as commands of enforcement (or protection), compelling the legislature to protect citizens among themselves. When this protection does not exist or is insufficient, judges must take this circumstance into account, *projecting the fundamental right on the relations between private individuals to provide the protection promised by the right, but forgotten by the law*.[27]

When there is this duty to protect and, therefore, that a suitable protective rule must be provided by the legislature, the absence of a normative shield can be argued before courts, to plead a remedy that makes up for the unconstitutional legislative omission. However, the provisions of fundamental rights do not stipulate the way,

[25] Cappelletti (1968), p. 62 et seq.

[26] Losano (2010), p. 245.

[27] Canaris *(*1989*), p. 161.*

shape or intensity with which an individual must be protected against another. Fundamental rights, by creating the State's general duty to protect, do not say "how" such protection should be carried out. To think about "how" the State should protect fundamental rights is the same as defining the measures that the State must necessarily adopt to enforce those rights. The constitution, at best, offers fragmented provisions about remedies that should be applied to safeguard fundamental rights.

It should be stressed that the decision on how a duty of enforcement must be fulfilled is, above of all, a question for parliament.[28] When legislators violate a fundamental right, which is seen, in this scenario, as a command of enforcement, it is up to courts to act insofar as to ensure that the duty of protection meets *the minimum requirements of efficiency*.[29] We must see that, more than to answer to a duty of enforcement, the judiciary acts to *ensure the control of the insufficient protection owed by the legislature*. In fact, this control logically pressuposes, in judicial argumentative reasoning, the duty to protect, in the sense that courts, to control insufficiency, ought to first determine if there is a duty to protect and what exactly legislation ought to provide under the minimal legal-constitutional requeriments. Only after this will courts define the means that, though protecting the fundamental right, do not exceed the minimum necessary.

The control of insufficient statutory protection of fundamental rights, by requiring consideration of the meaning of the right and the extent of the State's duty to enforce it, as well as the definition of the medium that, supplying the omission of the legislature, adequately does it, constitutes a kind of decision that is obviously unthinkable to the classical positivist judge and, therefore, that is unpredictable by positivist standards.

A decision of this magnitude, because of its content, although it can me taken by any judge or ordinary court, cannot evade constitutional precedent established by a supreme court. This is due to the mere fact that it relates to the meaning of a fundamental right, the extent of the State's duty to enforcement it and, even more, to the appropriate medium of its enforcement—which in principle should have been determined by legislators.

---

[28] Hesse (1998), p. 279.

[29] Canaris warns that, in private law, interests that can be safeguarded as fundamental rights are often in conflict. When legislators protect the wielder of a fundamental right, they, consequently, intervene, often and at the same time, in the position of another wielder of a fundamental right. Judicial review, therefore, is typically directed towards two orientations*: on the one hand, protection should not be limited to the constitutional minimum core; on the other, it should not be excessive, that is, it should not exceed what is proportional and necessary, interfering with the fundamental rights of other private individuals. In the original:* "'Die verfassungsrechtlich Prüfung geht folglich typischerweise in zwei Richtungen'. einerseits darf der Schutz nicht hinter dem verfassungsrechtliche gebotenen Minimum zurückbleiben, andererseits darf nicht 'übermäßig', d. h. mehr als erforderlich und verhältnismäßig, in die Grundrechte des anderen Privatrechtssubjekt eingreifen." Canaris (1989), p. 164.

3.4 General Clauses

It was not the possibility of judicial action supplying protection of rights ignored by legislators or the power to define the meaning of fundamental rights—using arguments that are not contemplated by legal rules—to invalidate laws, or to give them constitutionally compatible interpretation, that undermined positivism and the kind of predictability it offered.

The view that certain "conclusions" depend on the specific circumstances of concrete situations and historical moments made legislators understand that, towards such cases, they should enact provisions that have vague or indeterminate concepts or give judges the explicit power to complete the legal text, choosing the most suitable option to fairly solve the case. Such standards, called general clauses, are the result of a legislative technique distinguished from the casuistic technique. The latter is used when legislators provide criteria to legally qualify facts. General clauses, on the other hand, are characterized by vague or imprecise concepts, with the goal of allowing the treatment of concrete and new situations, which were not predictable nor existent at the time the rule was drafted.[30]

Facing a general clause, judges have the power to fashion the appropriate rule to regulate the case; the clause is a legislative text that consciously gives them a wide margin of participation in the creation of the legal rule. The technique of the general clauses is premised on the idea that legislation is insufficient and, in this sense, is an element that requires complementation by the judge.

Franz Wieacker, in his important *História do Direito Privado Moderno*, when looking at the formative process of the *Bürgerliches Gesetzbuch* (German Civil Code), warned that the reversal to general clauses has long been noticed. If judges' dogmatic discipline becomes too rigorous, they try to run towards general clauses (Hedemann), towards a jurisprudence focused exclusively on justice and free from obedience to principles. In times of injustice, general clauses apply political and ideological pressure over jurisprudence and political opportunism. Even if we disregard these degenerate times, general clauses allow the judge to enforce biased, personal valuations, their natural law frenzy or moralizing tendencies of the same nature against the letter and the spirit of the legal order. On the other hand, the inadequate use, increasingly frequent nowadays, of general clauses by the legislature gives judges a social responsibility that does not stem from their office. All these manifestations are based on the fact that general clauses do not allow and at the same time render meaningless any substantive activity, since it, in turn, does not refer to a well-defined situation of established morality and firm judicial technique. *While the theory of law and judicial tradition do not develop a technique that mirrors the correct use of general clauses, they will remain a growing threat to our legal system.*[31]

Surely, the technique of open clauses has given judges a space they had not and that, because of it, must draw attention from legal theory to avoid the multiplication

---

[30] See Picardi (2004), p. 46.

[31] Wieacker (1980), pp. 476–477.

of legal standards for the same cases, thus losing predictability and the violating equality. In fact, John Henry Merryman warns, in a study of comparative law about the civil law tradition, that it is not required too much imagination to see that clauses like good-faith give judges a great deal of undefined equitable power, leaving them almost unexposed to accountability before the legislative formula and distant from the ideal of judgeship conceived in the civil law tradition.[32]

Wieacker's concern finds an answer on the rationality of the argument that should govern the justification of decisions based on general clauses and, especially, on the need of this justification to come from a supreme court, which is responsible for determining how a general clause should be applied to certain specific circumstances that appear in similar cases.

Only respect to supreme court precedents can make it clear that general clauses are supposed to give the judiciary the power to fashion a rule of general application, albeit concerned with a specific circumstance that was not contemplated at the time of the enactment of the legal text. That is, the judicial rule derived from the legislative technique of general clauses, nevertheless it is based on a condition that has only just appeared in a concrete case, must have a universalizing character, given that it will have no rationality if it cannot be applied to future cases marked by the same circumstances.[33]

The scholars of the common law have noticed, when looking at civil law, that, in decisions about constitutional questions or about the application of general clauses, it is not possible to admit the distinction between interpretive precedent and solution precedent. They hold, in such cases, that the interpretation has such a wide scope and is guided by such fragile and vague arguments about the written law that the decision could be explained by both the interpretive theory and the positivist theory of judicial creation of law.[34]

This means, in other words, that decisions of civil law judges, at least when addressing constitutional matters or the use of general clauses, are related to predictability in the same way that are common law decisions, which implies that in our reality, which coexists with the correction of legislation according to fundamental rights by any judge or ordinary court and with the increasingly widespread use of open clauses, we cannot postpone the theorization of a mandatory system of precedent, able to give due authority to the decisions of the supreme courts, i.e. the Superior Court of Justice and the Supreme Federal Court.

[32] Merryman (2007), p. 53: "It is true that the legislature has acted and that its action is expressed as a substantive rule of law, but the terms are so broad ('good faith', which is not defined in the code, has an almost unlimited area of potential application) that the judge is hardly constrained by the legislative formulation. What that stature means depends on what judges do with it in concrete cases. What they do with it in concrete cases becomes the law in fact, although not in theory."

[33] In fact, by a logical and argumentative perspective, each and every decision must be universalizable; otherwise, they will not be justified from the point of view of the legal system. See Marinoni (2019), pp. 106–109; Mitidiero (2014), pp. 82–86. General clauses make this need for universalization even more sensitive.

[34] Bankowski et al. (1997), p. 485.

3.5 The Evolution of the Interpretation Theory

In the civil law tradition, judicial decisions are as stable and secure as legislation, and we may even say that it is legislation that decides the case.[35] The legal values that guide judicial decisions are certainty, stability and predictability. The theory of interpretation around the time of the French Revolution is called formalist or cognitive. Interpretation is considered a cognitive activity by nature and leads always to a description or plain statement.[36] According to this theory—which neighbours ideas of comprehensiveness and consistency of law—the content of the law is implicit in the legal text. Judges simply investigate and examine cases to declare what is already written in the text. The interpreter is bound by an existing standard. Therefore, the result of interpretation is a mere descriptive statement, subject to the test of truth and falsehood.

This theory of interpretation argues that the exact meaning of the law can and must always be found and that supreme courts have the function of correcting the legality of decisions. This theory is still kicking in civil law legal systems.

However, the evolution of interpretation theory made us see that the interpreter evaluates and choses one among many different possible interpretive results.[37] The rule, therefore, is not implied by the legal text, i.e. it does not precede interpretation, but rather derives from it.[38] The rule, as a judicial decision, is reconstructed from textual and extratextual elements of the legal order.[39] To do so, the judge engages in active evaluation, whether by choosing certain interpretative directive or by choosing one of the results of this interpretation-activity.[40] Guastini demonstrates that the common belief in the biunivocal correspondence between provision (or rule) and the rule's formulation is deceptive, because every provision is (more or less) vague and ambiguous, tolerating different and conflicting assignments of meaning. In this regard, to every provision—to each provision—corresponds not only one rule, but a plurality of dissociated rules. One provision dissociatedly expresses more rules: one or the other rule, depending on the several possible interpretations.[41]

The evolution of the interpretation theory puts in the hands of supreme courts the role of assigning meaning to law (or defining the proper interpretation of a legal text), underscoring the need for court decisions to be justified by rational arguments. Interpretative choices must be justified by rationally acceptable arguments.[42] Decisions can no longer be situated in the search for the exact meaning of the law

---

[35] Wróblewski (1973–1974), p. 322.

[36] Guastini (2011), p. 409.

[37] Wróblewski (2008), p. 136 et seq; Jori and Pintore (1995), p. 205 et seq.; Dicioti (1999), p. 200 et seq.; Sacco (1998), p. 111 et seq.

[38] Tarello (1980), pp. 63–64.

[39] Guastini (2009), p. 395; Ávila (2014), pp. 51–55.

[40] Wróblewski (1988).

[41] Guastini (2011), p. 65 et seq.

[42] Wróblewski (1974), p. 35 et seq.; Michelman (1986); Zaccaria (1996), pp. 3–20; Chiassoni (2007).

and become an instance to justify interpretive choices, i.e. to justify the rationality of interpretation. Law is, thus, interpretation and argumentative practice and, in this sense, gains autonomy from legislation.

Supreme court decisions, by expressing the meaning of the law, began to guide social life and the decisions of judges and appellate courts. If supreme courts have the responsibility of developing law alongside the legislature, their decisions should receive the authority that allows them to match their significance for the legal system. It is for this reason that supreme court decisions take on the quality of precedent.

It turns out that, despite the evolution of interpretation theory, the template of a court associated with interpretive formalism survived and is still present in Brazil and, to a greater or lesser degree, in almost all systems of civil law. We must note that when the role of the highest court comes down to state the exact meaning of the law, nothing is added to legislation and, hence, there is no way to have a decision that reveals meaning assigned to the legal text and, therefore, there is no reason to have authoritative precedents. If the court's decision simply tells us the *exact meaning of the law*, it is enough to have a system that ensures the correction of decisions that contradict *it*, directed towards the past.

However, when the court's decision *assigns meaning* to the law—because of the belief in the separation between text and rule—it provides unity in the law through the formation of precedents. To proclaim interpretation through precedent and, thereby, to ensure the unity of law is the duty of supreme courts, which means that "uniform interpretation" can no longer be a measure to control legality and should be regarded as synonymous with "unity of law". To better explain: uniform interpretation was a means to control legality, and precedent is a means to protect equality, to the extent that interpretation is no longer the method to reveal the rule contained by the legal text, but rather an instrument to compose its meaning. Consequently, a supreme court can only be seen as a court of interpretation that, by giving meaning to law, guarantees equality before it as a mere consequence.

All this means that, despite the evolution of interpretation theory and the possibility to theoretically understand the real role of supreme courts, it is still necessary to give them their due place, by awarding them the organization and the structure that would allow them to properly exercise their functions in a legal order struck by interpretive disputes and by the need to optimize stability and predictability.

References

Alexy R (2001) Los derechos fundamentales en el estado constitucional democrático. In: Los fundamentos de los derechos fundamentales. Trotta

Ascarelli T (1957) Giurisprudenza costituzionale e teoria dell'interpretazione. Rivista di diritto processuale 12:351–364

Ávila H (2014) Teoria dos Princípios. Malheiros

Bankowski Z, MacCormick N, Morawski L, Miguel AR (1997) Rationales for precedent. In: Interpreting precedents: a comparative study. Dartmouth

Canaris CW (1989) Grundrechtswirkungen und *Verhältnismäßigkeitsprinzip* in der richterlichen Anwendung und Fortbildung des Privatrechts. JuS 161–172
Cappelletti M (1968) Il controllo giudiziario di costituzionalità delle leggi nel diritto comparato. Giuffrè
Cappelletti M (2001) Repudiando Montesquieu? A expansão e a legitimidade da justiça constitucional. *Revista da Faculdade de Direito da Universidade Federal do Rio Grande do Sul*, 20: 261–286
Chiassoni P (2007) Tecnica dell'interpretazione giuridica. Il Mulino
Chiassoni P (2009) L'Indirizzo analitico nella filosofia del diritto. I. Da Bentham a Kelsen. Giappichelli
Chiassoni P (2011) Disposición y norma: una distinción revolucionaria. In: Disposición. vs norma. Palestra
Corwin ES (1910) The establishment of judicial review. Mich Law Rev 9:102–125
Crisafulli V (1964) Disposizione (e norma). Enciclopedia del diritto. Giuffrè 13:195–209
Dicey AV (1959) Introduction to the study of the law of the constitution, 10th edn. Macmillan
Dicioti E (1999) Interpretazione della legge e discorso razionale. Giappichelli
Ferrajoli L (2001) Derechos fundamentales. In: Los fundamentos de los derechos fundamentales. Trotta
Guastini R (1989) Disposizione vs. Norma. Giurisprudenza costituzionale 34:3–14
Guastini R (2009) Se i giudici creino diritto. In: Istituzioni e dinamiche del diritto. Giuffrè
Guastini R (2011) Interpretare e argomentare. Giuffrè
Häberle P (1972) Leistungsrecht im sozialen Rechtsstaat, Recht und Staat – Festschrift für K. Küchenhoff. Duncker & Humblot
Habermas J (1997) Direito e democracia. Tempo Brasileiro
Hazard GC Jr (1985) Reflections on the substance of finality. Cornell Law Rev 70:646–647
Hespanha AM (2012) Cultura jurídica europeia. Almedina
Hesse K (1998) Elementos de direito constitucional da República Federal da Alemanha. Fabris Editor
Irti N (1999) L'Età della decodificazione. Giuffrè
Irti N (2005) Codice Civile e società politica, 7th edn. Laterza
Jori M, Pintore A (1995) Manuale di teoria generale del diritto. Giappichelli
Larenz K (2012) Metodologia da Ciência do Direito (Lamêgo J, Trans.). Fundação Calouste Gulbekian
Losano MG (2010) Sistema e estrutura no direito, vol 2. Martins Fontes
Marinoni LG (2019) O STJ enquanto Corte de Precedentes, 4th edn. Thomson Reuters
Merryman JH (2007) The civil law tradition: an introduction to the legal systems of Europe and Latin America. Standford University Press
Michelman F (1986) Justification (and justifiability) of law in a contradictory world. Nomos XXVIII: Justification 71:71–99
Mitidiero D (2014) Cortes Superiores e Cortes Supremas. Thomson Reuters
Montesquieu (1973) Do espírito das leis. Abril Cultural
Picardi N (2004) La vocazione del nostro tempo per la giurisdizione. Rivista trimestrale di diritto e procedura civile 58:41–72
Pierlingieri P (1991) Il diritto civile nella legalità costituzionale. Edizioni Scientifiche Italiane
Rosenfeld M (2001) The rule of law and the legitimacy of constitutional democracy. South Calif Law Rev 74:1307–1351
Sacco R (1998) Interpretazione del diritto. Dato oggettivo e spirito dell'interprete. In Diritto, giustizia e interpretazione. Laterza
Scheuner U (1971) Die Funktion der Grundrechte im Sozialstaat. Die Grundrechte als Richtlinie und Rahmen der Staatstätigkeit. Die öffentliche Verwaltung – DÖV 24:505–513
Schmitt C (1982) Teoría de la constitución. Alianza
Sunstein C (1993) The partial constitution. Harvard University Press

Tarello G (1966) Il "problema" dell'interpretazione: una formulazione ambigua. Rivista internazionale di filosofia del diritto 43:349–357
Tarello G (1976) *Storia della cultura giuridica moderna* (assolutismo e codificazione del diritto). Il Mulino
Tarello G (1980) L'interpretazione della legge. Giuffrè
Wieacker F (1980) História do Direito Privado moderno (Privatrechtsgeschichte der Neuzeit unter besonderer Berücksichtigung der deutschen Entwicklung). Tradução de Antônio Manuel Hespanha. Fundação Calouste Gulbenkian
Wróblewski J (1973–1974) Functions of law and legal certainty. Anuario de Filosofia del Derecho 17:307–324
Wróblewski J (1974) Legal syllogism and rationality of judicial decision. Rechtstheorie. Duncker & Humblot 5:35
Wróblewski J (1988) Transparency and doubt. Understanding and interpretation in pragmatics and in Law. Law Philos 7:203–224
Wróblewski J (2008) Lenguaje jurídico e interpretación jurídica. In: Sentido y hecho en el derecho. Fontamara
Zaccaria G (1996) Complessità della ragione giuridica. In: Questioni di interpretazione, Cedam
Zagrebelsky G (1992) Il diritto mite. Einaudi
Zagrebelsky G (2003) A lei, o direito e a constituição (*Legislation, the law and the constitution*). Commemorative Colloquium on the 20th Anniversary of the Portuguese Constitutional Court. Lisbon
Zagrebelsky G (2005) Historia y constitución. Trotta

Chapter 4
Personalism, Patrimonialism, Cult of Irrationality and Contempt for Predictability in Brazil

Contents

This chapter shows a link between the irrationality and unpredictability of law and the underlying values embedded in the formative process of Iberic culture. Based on concepts by Max Weber and Buarque de Holanda, it suggests that the current lack of respect towards supreme courts' precedents derives from a culture characterized by personalism and patrimonialism. The aversion to impersonality and rationality, a feature of agents that seek to turn the public sphere into a private one and to run away from legislation's generality, results in a culture that does not adequately care about the predictability of the law and equality in judicial decisions.

L. G. Marinoni, *Culture and Predictability of Law*, SpringerBriefs in Law, https://doi.org/10.1007/978-3-031-87161-0_4

4.1 Rationality and Predictability in Contemporary Brazilian Law

Considering the reality of Brazilian civil justice, it seems clear that litigating parties experience great difficulty in predicting how a question of law will be decided. This is due to the fact that judges and courts do not comply with minimal patterns of rationality in their decisions. It is obvious that the use of general clauses and the adoption of constitutional principles to interpret legal rules, by themselves, broadened the scope of judicial power or the presence of subjectivity in the adjudication of cases. After all, judges, on the one hand, are called to decide on matters left unresolved by legislators and, on the other, have the power to deny the enforcement of legal rules that violate the constitution or to harmonize them with constitutional provisions. However, even when they have to simply enforce a rule, judges are faced with the duty to evaluate and decide or choose, which means they have to draw on, in any case, rational argumentative reasons. Only rational arguments constitute acceptable justification.[1]

Frequently, even in judicial decisions that merely enforce legal rules, there is little regard for explaining the reasons that justify the choice for a particular interpretive path. In fact, judges commonly offer no reasons to justify the evaluative choices they made throughout their reasoning. It is as if, despite deciding based on evaluations, judges cover them up with arguments that refer only to the literal legal text and to doctrinal and jurisprudential citations that have nothing to say about the choices implicitly made in the decision. There is no argument strong enough to convince, to make the decision rationally acceptable. Such acceptance, of course, is related to public opinion and, especially, to the parties of the case.[2]

In fact, Brazilian judicial practice shows that, nevertheless it is based on the premise that the act of deciding is not simply revealing the rule contained by the legal text, providing reasons for a decision has not yet become an exercise in rational argument to justify decisional choices—including the final decision—that have been made through the course of the judge's decisional reasoning. That is to say, if judges have the power to draw the law from the legal text through interpretation, there is still a long way to go before the law becomes an argumentative practice and, because of this, before it becomes rational and legitimate.

In any event, rational argument does not supply the need for another kind of rationality, one that relates to the application of the law by the judiciary. The judicial system, internally, has bodies that are responsible for eliminating interpretive doubts, precisely because it is incoherent and irrational to apply "multiple laws" in the face of conflicting cases. It is up to the Brazilian Supreme Federal Court, through extraordinary appeals, and to the Superior Court of Justice, through special appeals, to define, respectively, the meaning of the constitution and of regular federal law,

[1] On the subject, based on the doctrine of the Roman-canonical tradition, see Tarello (1980), Guastini (2011), Chiassoni (2007), Taruffo (1975).

[2] Taruffo (1975), p. 371; Cadiet et al. (2013), p. 685.

which ought to result in the expression of a rule that is autonomous in face of the text and that, consequently, is incorporated into the legal system. Now, a judicial system that allows, despite the intervention of its supreme courts, differing interpretations is completely incapable of fulfilling its duty of delivering "justice" in concrete cases. Such a system fails to ensure coherence in the legal order, equality before the law, freedom and predictability. In addition, it does not comprise a method of developing the law rationally and gradually as it faces new cases that require new legal solutions. Disrespect to supreme courts' precedent is an open door to an uneven and random delivery of "justice", with all its perverse consequences.

In Brazil, a significant number of trial and appellate judges in state and federal courts fail to respect or apply precedents established by the supreme courts. These judges and courts do not even provide arguments for doing so. Even worse, the Supreme Federal Court and the Superior Court of Justice themselves sometimes reach different conclusions in identical cases. This happens not only when one of their panels decides differently from the others, but also when the same panel, not rarely, does not follow one of their own previous decisions. This happens because both supreme courts still behave as courts of cassation, charged with correcting the decisions of lower courts, i.e. as courts of control and jurisprudence. They still do not look like courts of interpretation and precedent, which define the interpretation or the rule that ought to govern future cases, including those that reach their benches.

Additionally, although the extraordinary appeal to the Supreme Federal Court requires the constitutional question to have "general repercussion"—which is an evidence that it should be a court of precedent—there are still debates about the compulsory efficacy—also called binding—of the decisions rendered on those appeals. Some have argued that the only binding decisions would be those taken on cases of direct constitutional control, which is obviously absurd, especially because the only binding thing, in their view, would be the decision's determination or final judgment.

It is interesting to compare the Brazilian system of diffuse constitutional control or judicial review, tied to the absence of any binding effect of constitutional precedents, to the American system. It is true that in the United States, the concept of constitutional precedent did not come up at the same time as of the conception of the theory of judicial review of legislation. However, control of constitutionality, in Brazil, besides not being subject of in-depth debate in the legal community—it derived from the personal efforts of Rui Barbosa—has seen its meaning and consequences simply ignored by society. Or rather, here the idea of constitutional control owes nothing to societal values, differently from what took place in the United States.[3]

The saying that "*all laws which are repugnant to the Constitution are null and void*" does not depict the result of a simple exercise in logic structured around pyramidal ideas, since the constitution, to the settlers and to the founders of American

[3] On the values of American Society, see Chase (2005), p. 47 et seq. Also refer to Kagan (2001), p. 99 et seq.

constitutionalism, had a significance that transcended legal boundaries.[4] American constitutionalism is the first written constitutional experience, at the side of some Calvinist-inspired English experiences. As noted by Fernando Rey Martínez, the traditional American emphasis on a written constitution owes much to the Puritan insistence on *higher law* being *written law*.[5] The Puritan settlers not only reproduced Calvin's theory, in the sense that the law had to be written, *lex scripta*—seen as proof of the natural law[6]—but they also had in mind the experience of the Reformation, marked by the affirmation of the Bible's text as means to free men from the "divine power" created by the Catholic Church. We should remember that one of the most important Puritan victories on English soil occurred in 1628, when the famous *Petition of Rights* was imposed upon Charles I, which clearly undescored the Calvinist theory of a higher law that subjected both the legislature and the judiciary.[7]

This means that, if the idea of constitutional precedent took some time to emerge in the United States, this is probably due to the deliberate caution with which the constitution was enforced.[8] The constitution, given its nature as a supreme law, almost sacred in character, should be enforced literally, leaving no room for the judiciary to apply rules that are in conflict with it. However, when there are signs of interpretive doubt, the logic of the authority of supreme court precedent turns up in full force, because, after all, judicial review of legislation has an intrinsically unifying force of the law, to the extent that, in a system of mutual control between the

[4] See Levinson (1988).

[5] Martínez (2003), p. 55 et seq. Wood notes that "just like all Englishmen, the colonists were familiar with written documents as barriers to unlimited power". Wood (1998), p. 268.

[6] The Declaration of Independence, adopted by the Continental Congress on July 4, 1776, refers, in its first paragraph, to the "Laws of Nature" as a reason for the act of political separation between the American colonies and England. Next, it affirms: "We hold these truths to be self-evident, that all men are created equal, that they are endowed by their Creator with certain unalienable Rights, that among these are Life, Liberty and the pursuit of Happiness. That to secure these rights, Governments are instituted among Men, deriving their just powers from the consent of the governed. That whenever any Form of Government becomes destructive of these ends, it is the Right of the People to alter or to abolish it, and to institute new Government." The acceptance of the principles of natural law is explicit, especially according to John Locke's proposition: "when one or more persons take unto themselves the creation of laws, not being legitimately appointed by 'the people's' choice, hence these persons create law without the authority of doing so, consequently, 'the people' are not obliged to obey such laws; in such conditions, 'the people' are again not obliged to submit themselves to it, and are entitled to constitute a new legislature as they deem appropriate, having complete freedom to resist the enforcement of those who, without authority, want to impose any thing unto them." Locke (1980), p. 80.

[7] Martínez (2003), pp. 57–61.

[8] The framers, despite having had experience with common law precedent, certainly has no knowledge of constitutional precedent, that is, precedent that serve to interpret constitutional provisions. Constitutional adjudication was something totally new. The theory of the constitutional precedent requires, at least, the beginnings of a discussion about constitutional interpretation. In 1958, in *Cooper v. Aaron* (358 U.S. 1 (1958)), the Supreme Court held: "The interpretation of the Fourteenth Amendment enunciated by this Court in the Brown case is the supreme law of the land, and Art. VI of the Constitution makes it of binding effect on the States." See Gerhardt (2008), p. 48 et seq.

branches of government—checks and balances—one cannot conceive the fragmentation of what is said by the judiciary—miscellaneous judicial decisions about the validity of laws.

In Brazil, many judges still believe they can assign meaning to the texts that consecrate fundamental rights as they please—as if the Constitution were an outlet to express their own personal values and desires—and, thus, decide without any commitment to constitutional precedent, in a clear demonstration of their noninstitutional thought.

Behind this disrespect for precedent are rhetorical legal arguments, cultural values and even a clear interest in an inconsistent legal system that is subject to sudden changes. It is important to understand that the lack of authority of supreme court decisions derives not only from the theoretical rejection of the idea that they must determine the meaning of the law and, therefore, guide other courts, but also from the indifference of people holding significant social positions in the rationalization of the distribution of the law in the country.

When looking at things properly, we see multiple key position-holders in markets, as well as in government, plus a number of judges and some lawyers themselves, interested in inconsistency and irrationality than in otherwise. This topic, though never unovered before, has great relevance in civil law countries with cultures that are averse to rationality and impersonality in public administration, including the administration of justice.

4.2 The Impact of Counter-Reformation Values in Iberian Countries and in the Colonization of America

The Reformation, led by Luther and later by Calvin, showed deviations from the Catholic Church, which, instead of spreading the faith, had become a vehicle for manipulating political and economic power. The Reformation emphasized, among other things, the importance of reading the Bible as a means to demystify the dogmas of the Church and stressed the invalidity of the sacraments of salvation as well as the concept of work as a means of salvation, both of which served to strengthen the Church politically and economically.

Calvinists eventually came to understand that *proof* of salvation would be born through the *rational* control of the acts performed within mundane life. The sacraments of salvation and the works became viewed as magic. In this sense, the Reformation has allowed men to rationalize their lives and, consequently, the social groups they are a part of as well as society as a whole. Hence, the Reformation has given rise—as demonstrated by Weber in *The Protestant Ethic and the Spirit of Capitalism*—to a way of life centered on inner-worldly asceticism, from which stems the concept of work as a religious duty, thus stimulating the development of capitalism and of the need for a legal system endowed with formal rationality, to which predictability was inherent.

Rome and its Latin allies felt the need to respond to the attacks of the Protestant Reformation. The resistance of the papacy to a mediation led Rome to manipulate a Council that became inevitable—called the Council of Trent—whence came the so-called Counter-Reformation, an absolutist choice that strengthened the orthodoxy and stiffened the discipline of the Church, establishing values that were *responsible for the decay of the peninsular peoples.*

The *Catholicism* established by the Council of Trent, in essence, rejected the great achievement of the Reformation: *the moral freedom that led to the examination of the individual consciousness, responsible for the strong emphasis on personal responsibility,* which was essential to the posture assumed by Protestants in their lives. The Council of Trent *condemned human reasoning and free thought,* considering them as crimes against God. The Catholic prohibition against reading the Bible, for example, is nothing more than qualifying human reasoning as sin and to question the cognitive ability of mankind, forcing men to have a way of life guided by the knowledge of a few enlightened people.

The impossibility of questioning religious dogmas and the magic solution from the sacraments of salvation, like confession, did not stimulate the examination of conscience to investigate personal responsibility but, instead, eliminate the reason for a life guided by a rational agenda.

Antero de Quental, in a speech in Lisbon in 1871, argued that the Catholicism established by the Council of Trent not only was a major contributor to the decline of the peninsular peoples in the seventeenth, eighteenth and nineteenth centuries but also had adverse effect on colonization on American soil:

> And to us, Spanish and Portuguese, how was that Catholicism nullified us? Catholicism weighed on us from all sides, with all its weight. With the Inquisition, an invisible terror hangs over Society: hypocrisy becomes a national and necessary vice: denunciation is a religious virtue: the expulsion of Jews and Moors impoverished both nations, paralyzes commerce and industry, and gives mortal blow to agriculture throughout southern Spain: the persecution of New Christians made capital disappear: the Inquisition crosses the sea, and, making us hostile to the Indians, preventing the fusion of the conquerors and the conquered, makes the establishment of solid and lasting colonization impossible: in America it depopulates the Antilles, terrifies the indigenous populations, and makes the Christian name a symbol of death; religious terror, finally, corrupts the national character and turns two generous nations into hordes of hardened fanatics, the horror of civilization. With Jesuitism, Christian sentiment disappears, giving way to the most deplorable sophisms to which religious consciousness has ever descended: teaching methods, at the same time brutal and refined, sterilize intelligence, targeting memory, *with the aim of killing inventive thinking, and manage to alienate the peninsular spirit from the great movement of modern science, essentially free and creative: Jesuit education turns the elevated classes into intelligent and passive machines*; *the people into corrupt and cruel fanatics*: the deadly Jesuit morality, explained (and practiced) by its casuists, *with its mental restrictions*, its subtleties, its mistakes, its condescension, infiltrates everywhere, like a slow poison, morally disorganizes society, undoes the spirit of family, *corrupts consciences with the continuous oscillation of the notion of duty*, and annihilates characters, softens them, turns them into sophisms: the ideal of Jesuit education is a people of *mute, obedient and imbecile children*, realized in the famous missions of Paraguay; Paraguay was the kingdom of heaven of the Society of Jesus; perfect order, perfect devotion; only one thing was missing, the soul, that is, dignity and will, which distinguishes

man from animality! These were the benefits we brought to the savage races of America, by the civilizing hands of the Society's priests! That is why the free popular genius declined, fell asleep everywhere: in art, in literature, in religion.

(...)

There is, in fact, something fatal in the reprehensible acts of the peninsular peoples, in the errors of their politics, and in the decadence that brought them about: it is the law of historical evolution, which inflexibly and impassively draws the consequences from the principles once introduced into society. Given absolute Catholicism, it was impossible not to follow, deducing from it, monarchical absolutism. Given absolutism, the aristocratic spirit necessarily came, *with its procession of privileges, injustices, with the predominance of warrior tendencies over industrial ones. The political and economic mistakes came out of here naturally; and from all of it, through the transgression of the law of social life, decadence in all forms also naturally emerged.* And these false social conditions did not only produce the effects I pointed out. They produced another one, which, being invisible and insensitive, nevertheless remains the most fatal. It is the dejection, the prostration of the national spirit, perverted and atrophied by a few centuries of the most harmful education. The causes I have indicated have largely ceased: *but the moral effects persist*, and it is to them that we must attribute the uncertainty, the discouragement, and the malaise of our contemporary society. *To the influence of the Catholic spirit, in its heavy dogmatism, must be attributed this universal indifference towards philosophy, science, moral and social modern movement, this somnambulistic numbness in the face of the revolution of the 19th century, which is almost our characteristic and national feature among the peoples of Europe. We certainly no longer believe, with the passionate and blind ardor of our grandparents, in Catholic dogmas: but we continue to close our eyes to the truths discovered by free thought.*[9]

Tridentine Catholic values are not only distinct from those of Calvinism. They had *opposite* effects on the way men carry their personal lives and, therefore, on the development of society. While Catholicism forbade free thought and made men dependent on the Church—for example, by compelling confession to priests, prescribed in Section 14 of the Council of Trent—Calvinism, based on God's sovereign will and on predestination, forced men to look for signs of salvation in daily acts of life, especially in the exercise of one's profession, which required the *rationalization* of one's way of life, along with the methodical investigation of consciousness and a very strong feeling of *personal responsibility*.

4.3 Patrimonialism in the Formation of Brazilian Culture: From Weber to Buarque de Holanda

Sérgio Buarque de Holanda, in the classic *Roots of Brazil*,[10] analyses the foundations and fundamentals of our history according to Weber's typological criterion.[11] Buarque de Holanda uses two ideal types (e.g. a hard worker and an adventurer,

---

[9] Quental (1871).

[10] Holanda (1995).

[11] For Weber, ideal types, outlined based on deliberate exaggeration of features of the investigated phenomenon, are tools to analyze reality.

impersonality and emotional impulse, etc.) to, by comparing and contrasting them, explain matters that are greatly important to understanding our historical destiny.[12]

In the famous chapter titled "The Cordial Man", Holanda employs the Weberian concepts of patrimonialism and bureaucracy. These concepts are employed to demonstrate the meaning of the "cordial man", a personal behavioural prototype representative of the formation of Brazilian culture, hostile to impersonality and to formal rationality and clearly related to the model of institutions and public administration in Brazil—a prototype that remains in the country's culture.[13]

It is important to recall that Weber, in analysing the legitimacy of different forms of domination, identified three principal foundations—conceptualized as ideal types—for legitimizing authority: (i) rational or legal-bureaucratic, (ii) traditional and (iii) charismatic. Traditional domination is founded in the belief in the lifelong sanctity of existing traditions and in the legitimacy of those who, by virtue of these traditions, represent authority (traditional domination).[14] This kind of authority, when contrasted with rational domination, has very clear characteristics. As Weber explains, rational domination is based on statutes, which results in subservience to an impersonal order, objectively established by law, and to the leaders legitimized by this order. In traditional domination, however, obedience is directed to the *master*, recognized as such by tradition, something that is done purely out of respect for customs.[15]

In traditional domination, the impersonality and rationality of the form of authority do not matter, unlike what happens in rational or legal-bureaucratic domination, not even the leader at one end of domination must be particularly charismatic—charismatic domination—since obedience is given to the person appointed by tradition and by customary habits.[16]

When speaking about traditional domination, Weber identifies as the primary types of authority gerontocracy and patriarchalism. In both, the master has no administrative staff. In gerontocracy, elders rule within a group, presumably because they possess a greater knowledge of tradition. In primary patriarchalism, authority is attributed to a subject based on the rules of succession and inheritance.[17]

---

[12] Antonio Candido (1995), p. 13.

[13] Holanda (1995, 2012).

[14] Weber (2004a), p. 141.

[15] In domination based on statutes, obedience is directed towards the impersonal, objective and legally established order and the superiors that it determines by virtue of the formal legality of its provisions and within the scope of their cogency. In the case of traditional domination, obedience is given to the master appointed by tradition and bound by it (within the scope of its cogency) by virtue of his devotion to customary habits. Id., p. 141.

[16] Portela (2012), p. 12.

[17] The primary types of traditional authority are cases where the leader has no personal administrative staff, i.e. (a) gerontocracy and (b) patriarchalism. The term gerontocracy is applied to a situation wherein, if there is some authority within the group, it is attributed to its elders (originally, in the literal sense of the word: because of age), because they are the best experts in the sacred tradition. Gerontocracy is often found in groups that are not primarily economic or family-like in nature. Patriarchalism represents a situation in which, within a (domestic) group, often primarily

The study of the types of primary patriarchalism and gerontocracy is important to understand the notion of patrimonialism. For Weber, only when the master begins to depend on the support of a personal administrative and military staff, will domination lean towards patrimonialism and, when the master's power is extreme, will it lean to sultanism.[18] The difference between patrimonialism and sultanism is fluid, and Weber designates as *patrimonial* the domination that is exercised by virtue of full personal legitimate rights.[19]

The essential feature of this ideal type is the personalism of the master's decisions, as indicated by the expression "full personal right", employed by Weber. For this reason, we can say that patrimonialism is a form of domination in which the master acts upon personal considerations without being subject to objective or impersonal criteria derived from statutes.

In patrimonialism, legitimacy—a ground for obedience—is based on a sacred authority that has existed since time immemorial. Its archetype is patriarchal authority. Because it is based on an atavistic and, at the same time, arbitrary and compassionate power of the patriarch, it is manifested in a personal and unstable manner, which depends on the whims and subjectivity of the dominator. The political community, which is an expansion of the domestic community, adopts from the latter, by analogy, the forms and, especially, the spirit of "piety" (the spirit of purely personal devotion to the sovereign or *pater*, which relates to reverence for the sacred and the traditional) to unite the dominant and the subordinates.[20]

As explained, unlike gerontocracy and primary patriarchalism, patrimonialism requires an administrative staff because once the domestic community—the foundation of patriarchalism—is decentralized, that is, once community members start to inhabit properties that are dependent on the patriarch's assistance, an organized administration and a group of employees become necessary (patrimonial functionalism).[21] This system, however, does not observe the separation between private and official capacities because the administration, in patrimonialist domination, concerns exclusively—it is the exclusive property of—the master. It is up to him, based on purely subjective criteria, to choose the members of his staff and define the scope of their roles. In patrimonialist functionalism, because positions are filled based on personal relationships and trust, neither the actual ability of the beneficiary nor the prior definition of their tasks matters. As Weber said, all service

economic and family-like in nature, authority is wielded by an individual (normally) determined by fixed rules of succession. Weber (2004a), p. 151.

[18] With the development of a purely personal administrative (and military) staff, traditional authority leans towards patrimonialism and, with an extreme degree of seigneurial power, towards sultanism. Id.

[19] It is called patrimonial all authority that, originally guided by tradition, is exercised by virtue of full personal right, and sultanist all patrimonialist authority that, with its forms of administration, is found, first, in the realm of arbitrary discretion, detached from tradition. The difference is entirely fluid. Ibidem.

[20] Campante (2003), p. 162.

[21] Portela (2012), p. 13.

orders that, according to our conception, are "regulations" constitute, therefore, along with all the public order of patrimonially governed States in general, the ultimate instance in a system of purely subjective rights and privileges of certain people, which stem from the grant and grace of the master. There is no objective order or objectivity aimed at the impersonal ends of State bureaucratic life. The office and the exercise of public power are at the *service of the master's person*, on the one hand, and of the *employee to whom the office was awarded*, on the other, and not at the service of "objective" tasks.[22]

It is important to reiterate that primary patriarchalism, gerontocracy, patrimonialism and sultanism are ideal types, which, as Weber himself pointed out, do not exist in historical reality.[23] They are, like all ideal types, instruments for observing reality. Therefore, when we speak of "patrimonialism", we refer to a form of domination based on personalism and, consequently, on the lack of objectivity and generality. In patrimonialism, decisions follow the personal criteria of the *master*, which completely ignores the impersonality that predominates in rational domination.

Therefore, when we link patrimonialism to the judiciary, we refer to the personal nature of decisions, prevalent in a system where there is no respect for the precedents of supreme courts.

Sérgio Buarque de Holanda, in the first five chapters of *Raízes do Brasil* (*Roots of Brazil*), establishes the several key points that explain how patrimonialism, and particularly the "cordial man", became embedded in Brazilian culture. In the first chapter, Holanda presents personalism, a trait of the Iberian peoples, and its influence on the lack of social cohesion and the apathy of organizations: it may be said, indeed, that due to the particular importance given to the self-worth of a person, Spaniards and Portuguese owe much of their national originality to the autonomy of each man when compared to others in time and space. For them, the measure of a man's value is determined, first, by the extent to which he does not depend on others, does not need anyone and is self-reliant. It is from this idea that the singular lukewarmness of the forms of organization largely stems, in all associations involving ordination and solidarity among these peoples. In a land where everyone is a baron, it is impossible to maintain a durable collective bargain, unless through a reputable and feared external force.[24]

In the second chapter, titled "Trabalho e Aventura" ("Work and Adventure"), Holanda presents a typology comparing the worker and the adventurer—two colliding ethics[25]—and demonstrates that the colonizer, considered an "adventurer", only wanted the immediate reward and easy money. What the Portuguese came to take was, without a doubt, wealth—wealth that demanded boldness, not one that required

---

[22] Weber (2004b), p. 255.

[23] The fact that none of the three ideal types, to be examined next, in more depth, usually exist historically in an actually "pure" form should not, on any occasion, prevent the definition of the concept in the purest form possible. Weber (2004a), p. 141.

[24] Holanda (1995), p. 32.

[25] Antonio Candido (1995), p. 14.

labour. Everyone wanted to pull from the ground excessive benefits without great sacrifice. In urban trades reigned the same love for easy profit and instability that so much define, in Brazil, rural work. Only a few individuals could dedicate their whole lives to only one profession without being lured by another apparently profitable trade. Even rarer were cases where a trade remained within the same family for more than one generation, as normally happened in lands where social stratification had reached a higher degree of stability.[26]

The important idea that the settlers, seen within the ideal type of the adventurer, despised work and personal effort that had no prospect of immediate results *and, consequently, the stability and predictability of social and commercial relations.* Well, if the goal is immediate and easy profit, and there is in society a singularly energic accent on the affective, the irrational, the passionate, and a stagnation rather a corresponding atrophy of ordering, disciplinary and rationalizing qualities,[27] not only *there is reason to worry about the calculability of social actions, but there is no incentive for the law to be rational or predictable.*

In the third chapter, the rural-urban dichotomy is introduced, and we are reminded, already in its first paragraph, that the whole structure of our colonial society was rooted outside of urban environments. The rural environment is defined as the place of the patriarchal family, which is widened through the presence of slaves and aggregates on plantations and households, which, in turn, extends the power of the pater-families. Holanda also shows that the image of the patriarchal family, marked by affection and by personal preferences, was projected over all social life, *contaminating the public space with its moods and feelings, which points to the absence of impersonality and of rationality in public administration and, therefore, to patrimonialism.*[28]

The fourth chapter, titled "O Semeador e o Ladrilhador" ("The Sower and the Tiler"), establishes a comparison between the Spanish and the Portuguese, arguing that the first—the tiler—drew planned cities, demonstrating an intention to give the

[26] Holanda (1995), pp. 49, 52, 58–59.

[27] Id., p. 61.

[28] In rural domains, it is the type of family organized according to the classic norms of the old Roman canonic law, established in the Iberian Peninsula through countless generations, which serves as the basis and centre of the entire organization. Plantation and domestic slaves, and, not just them, but also aggregate members, expand the family circle and, with it, the immense authority of the paterfamilias. This very singular nucleus in every way behaves like its model from antiquity, in which the word "family", itself derived from *famulus*, is closely linked to the idea of slavery, and in which even children are only the free members of the vast body, entirely subjected to the patriarch, the liberi. The family framework thus becomes so powerful and demanding that its shadow haunts individuals even outside their homes. The private entity always precedes the public one. The nostalgia for this compact, unique and non-transferable organization, where preferences based on emotional ties necessarily prevail, could not fail to mark our society, our public life, all our activities. Because it represented the only sector where the principle of authority is undisputed, the colonial family provided the most normal idea of power, respectability, obedience and cohesion among men. The result was that one's own feelings towards the domestic community, naturally particularistic and anti-political, dominated social life, an invasion of the public by the private, of the State by the family. Holanda (1995), pp. 81–82.

colonized land aspects of the metropolis, while the Portuguese, as sowers, allowed cities to emerge and develop without criteria, demonstrating a lack of care or concern for the colony.[29]

When examining the "cordial man", in the fifth chapter, Sérgio Buarque de Holanda draws on all the aforementioned elements to define the personality of the Brazilian man, outlining an ideal standard to help understand how he was introduced into social life as well as *the historical causes of the ills in our government—including the administration of justice*.

Because they are accustomed to the way of living in the family circle—in Weber's typology, in primary patriarchalism, converted into full patrimonialism after the introduction of an administrative staff—where relations of affection and mere preference take place, Brazilians, when faced with the outside world, cannot see it in an impersonal and rationalized manner, seeking to shape all relationships and places, especially public administration, based on affective and personalized criteria. At this point, the Brazilian man projects himself as a "cordial man", that is, as someone who does not tolerate impersonality and tries to reduce it at the cost of a merely apparent affective behaviour, insincere, which always seeks sympathy, personal benefits and amenities.[30]

It is at the precise moment when Holanda talks about the "cordial man" that he turns to the Weberian concepts of patrimonialism and bureaucracy. He points out how difficult it was for holders of important public offices, reared within the primitive environment of the patriarchal family, to *understand the fundamental distinction between the private and public domain*, which is why they are defined as "patrimonial" employees, as opposed to the pure bureaucrat officials, according to Max Weber's distinction.[31] After all, to the "patrimonial" employee, political management itself is a matter of his private interest; functions, jobs and benefits that are enjoyed are related to the *personal rights of the employee and not to objective interests, as it happens in the bureaucratic State, where specialized offices and the effort to ensure legal guarantees to citizens prevail*. Men are chosen to hold public office based on the *personal trust* earned by them *and not according to their own abilities*. In all, there is a lack of personal ordering that characterizes life in the bureaucratic State. Patrimonial functionalism can, with a progressive division of tasks and with rationalization, acquire bureaucratic features, but, in essence, this type of functionalism distances itself from bureaucratic functionalism the more they are put side by side.[32]

---

[29] Routine and not abstract reason was the principle that guided the Portuguese, in this as in so many other expressions of their colonizing activity. They preferred to act in successive experiences, not always coordinated with each other, rather than drawing up a plan in advance and following it to the end. Id., p. 109.

[30] As Holanda argues, the temperament of the average Brazilian admits 'formulas of reverence', so long as they do not suppress the possibility of family-like interactions. The normal manifestation of respect for other peoples is generally opposed in Brazilian culture by the desire to establish closeness. Holanda (1995), p. 148.

[31] Id., p. 146.

[32] Ibidem.

This means that the family environment, transposed to public life, leads the public employee and those he relates with to behave against impersonality and legal rationality. The public sphere is invaded by the winds of the familial circle, of private life, and the employee begins to act as if he held an office he ought to enjoy, even in favour of those who are close to him, who begin claim their own spoils and, curiously, also their real rights, always based on cordiality animated by gestures of sympathy and the pursuit of intimacy.

Holanda argues that only exceptionally Brazil has had an administrative system and a cohort of employees purely dedicated to objective interests and grounded on those interests. We can witness throughout our history the constant predominance of private wills that are proper to closed circles and inaccessible to impersonal ordering. Among these circles, the family was, undoubtedly, the one that achieved the strongest expression and development in our society. And one of the key deficiencies of the unquestionable, absorbent supremacy of the nuclear family—the space, par excellence, of the so-called primary contacts, of heart and blood ties—is that the relationships reared in domestic life have always provided the essential mandatory layout to any social composition between us. This happens even when democratic institutions, founded on neutral and abstract principles, seek to establish a society based on universal norms.[33]

This all certainly pervaded the administration of justice, leading, for example, to the formation of the famous "groups" in courts, that is, the ethics of the all-in-favour of fellow allies and, even worse, the manipulation of decisions in favour of those—including governments and individuals and corporations associated to political power—who have relationships with the people holding the offices. Undoubtedly, there is no reason to suppose that the administration of justice would not be contaminated by the logic and impulses that, since the dawn of our history, seem to indicate that the public space should be enjoyed not only in favour of the employee, but also of those who deserve his trust, or better, his esteem and sympathy.

There was and still is space for the "cordial man"—the judge and the prosecutor who act based on the old motives that presided over the patriarchal family when everything revolved around personality. Lawyers can also be under this outfit, when they become "grovelers" who cease to be defenders of rights to become a lobbyists for private interests, for which purpose having the relationships expressed by the sayings "find a way" (*jeitinho*) or "way" (*jeito*)[34] are more effective than technical and legal knowledge or the capacity to convince the judge.

---

[33] Ibidem.

[34] The *jeito* (find a way), or *arranjo* (arrangement), is a pleasant, often touching or even desperate social behavior of connecting the impersonal to the personal, of juxtaposing a personal problem with an impersonal one to solve the former using the latter as a ladder or ram. Normally, one calls on a personal relationship, stemming from regionality, taste, religion, and other factors that are external to the formal/legal bureaucratic problem to be faced, through which one obtains the sympathy of the representative of the State and, consequently, a satisfactory solution. The distance between the written law and its practical application makes of the "find a way" method of social conduct a highly sought paralegal institution in Brazil, an integral part of our culture, to the point that, in many areas of the law, it is the rule. The "find a way", to placate the rigor of the law, is

As a product of Brazilian patrimonialism, the "cordial man", dressed in the party, lawyer or judge, evidently prevented the equal enforcement of the law, since it is neutral and abstract only to those who do not have "good reasons"—that is, those who were not part of the "inner circle"—to be treated in an individualized manner. In fact, the logic of law enforcement, in a culture marked by patrimonialism and dominated by the citizen who responds to it—the "cordial man"—can only be that of the manipulated application and interpretation, well summarized in the known and popular saying: "to my friends, all; to my enemies, the law!" Note that this expression, whose authorship is controversial, though has certainly been a suitable description of the Brazilian environment for a long time, besides confirming the aversion of our culture to impersonality and rationality, becomes evidence that equality and, more clearly and specifically, the uniform application of the law have always been ghosts we have learned to live with in a world devoid of boundaries between what is public and what is private, based on the belief in the logic of "personal" relationships.

However, if universal rules are essential to a society that aspires to develop itself and not favour a select few, it is necessary to take a step back and think about who has always cared about and benefited from irrationality and what can be done to eliminate the chaos in which our justice is submerged. Simply put, we need to decide if we want to abandon the "find a way" standard of social practice in favor of the universality of the law and the proper authority of the judiciary as a public institution. In short, we need to decide if we want to be a "family" or a nation.

4.4 Culture of Personalism, Lack of Social Cohesion and Weak Institutions

One defining trait of the Iberian peoples is personalism—the exaltation of autonomy or the exclusive concern with individual affirmation and the lack of commitment to goals that do not specifically relate to personal interests.[35]

The culture of personalism is the opposite of associativism, in which the interests of the community prevail and amass de efforts of its participants on behalf of

potentialized by sentimentality, probably founded on the Catholic ethics of forgiveness, on the cultural tendency to conciliate, and on the proverbial "cordiality" of the average Brazilian. The "find a way" is the cordial variant of the "do you know who you are talking to" social practice, because both are founded on the network of personal relationships that buttress a trickster's (*malandro*) pretensions, whether he is cordial (makes use of the "find a way") or arrogant (can be the same person, after being frustrated in his attempt to an "arrangement"). In both cases, the egalitarian and impersonal formal structure is overcome by—for example—name-dropping relatives (find a way) or authorities ("do you know who you are talking to") and, hence, the circumvention of the law becomes an "honorable exception". In short, the mismatched application of the law happens to the taste of the "find a way" and to everyone's network of personal relationships. See Rosenn (1998), Damatta (1997, 2001).

[35] Holanda (1995), pp. 32–40.

achieving common goals. Associativism is motivated by solidarity, which, for some reason, encourages individuals to be concerned with their peers and with a common environment.

Community vision, focused on the realization of common goals, naturally contributes to social cohesion and, therefore, requires the organization of individual wills within the group. In other words, there is a relationship of solidarity, social cohesion and organization.

According to Sérgio Buarque de Holanda, theories that deny free will (e.g. predestination theories, Calvinist theories) have always been regarded with suspicion and antipathy by the Spanish and the Portuguese. This happens because, to the extent that these theories deny individual capacity to change what has been predestined by God, they cannot avoid being despised by the member os a personalist culture. The personalist mentality of the Spaniards and the Portuguese was the biggest obstacle to the spirit of spontaneous organization of Protestant peoples, especially Calvinists. In Iberian nations, in face of no rationalization of life, which had been experienced earlier in some Protestant lands, the unifying principle ended up being represented by governments. In these nations, the type of political organization artificially upheld by an external force predominated incessantly, something which, in modern times, is mostly illustrated by military dictatorships.[36]

We should remember, moreover, that Protestant asceticism, that is, the concern with the correction of the actions practiced in everyday life, gave work a peculiar connotation, because its performance in a dignified and adequate manner was a duty and represented proof of election.[37] However, inner-worldly asceticism was not solely related to a form of work focused on personal achievements. What mattered, after all, was the fulfilment of duties (among them work) indispensable for proving predestination.[38] These duties, associated to daily life, could not help but be con nected to the effort required to achieve the interests of the group or the community. Work, as a valued activity, is associated with solidarity, which encourages social cohesion and requires organization and order.

As underlined by Buarque de Holanda, a fact that cannot be overlooked in the examination of the psychology of the Iberian peoples is their invincible repulsion towards any morality founded on the cult of work. This disdain for the value of work leads to a reduced capacity for social organization. In effect, humble, anonymous and selfless effort is a powerful agent of the solidarity of interests and, as such, it encourages rational organization of men and sustains cohesion among them. Wherever any form of work ethics prevails, there will hardly be a lack of order and tranquillity among people because both are necessary to harmonize interests. On the other hand, among the Spanish and the Portuguese, the morality of work always

[36] Id., pp. 37–38.

[37] Weber (2004c), p. 72.

[38] Biéler (2012), p. 590.

represented an exotic fruit. It is no surprise that, among these people, the ideas of solidarity were precarious.[39]

The culture of personalism, by not allowing agreements and compromises in favour of the community, along with the contempt for the value of work, by discouraging rational organization for the benefit of "all", obstructed solidarity and social order. This inhibited social cohesion, undermining associativism aimed at the achievement of common interests.

In public administration, where offices were exercised for the benefit of employees and those with whom they are related, there was no opportunity to unite efforts to realize the institution's objective interests. Besides the institution being seen as a private space, the combination of efforts could only happen to reach the desires of those who episodically would organize themselves to achieve their personal interests, which obviously has nothing to do with the general interest that should guide them.

4.5 The Absence of Institutional Vision in the Exercise of the Judicial Function

The looseness of the judiciary—as an institution—also stems from the way through which Brazilians, since the beginning of their cultural formation, were introduced to the public space. Personalism and patrimonialism hampered association, social cohesion and strong institutions—in which, for example, a judge could see himself as someone who simply contributes to the proper administration of justice in the country and not as an individual who is free to do whatever he wants.

Personalism and patrimonialism, after they appeared in the formative process of Brazilian culture, never went away, to the extent that a culture is not disconnected from its roots, though the behaviors that arose from its formative elements may change over time.

Although one can also hint at the "cordial" exercise of the judicial function, wherein those who have relationships with the judge and with the power that support him are benefitted, what matters here is the individualistic fashion through which he performs his function within the institution to which he belongs. It is here that there is value to cohesion and ordination to achieve a common end. The difficulty to prioritize institutional ends causes individual wills to prevail, as if to reach the institution's end it is enough for everyone to perform each individual duty, that is, as if ordering the various wills and functions to accomplish institutional scopes did not matter.

Admittedly, a single judge can resolve one contentious case. However, adjudication does not aim to solve conflicts on an accidental and episodic fashion—for which purpose it would be enough to distribute power among different judges

[39] Holanda (1995), p. 39.

devoid of any commitment to the institution—but rather has a duty to provide relief in a consistent and isonomic style, without hurting predictability, which then requires a rational distribution of justice, or rather order within the institution's structure. Without a doubt, hierarchy is inherent to the realization of the ends of an institution composed of various "wills"—not caudillist hierarchy, which, incidentally, has always worked in Brazil, but hierarchy as rational organization, without which the institutional voice cannot be effectively expressed.

A system of distribution of justice is more branded by the will of the individual judge—and is, therefore, irrational—the less respect there is to the authority of its high courts. Of course, many civil law systems, stirred by other cultures, preserve the ordinary judge's power to decide in disagreement with supreme courts, but it is interesting to notice that, in our culture, not only it is unreservedly defended the right of a judge to decide according to his own conviction, but there are also efforts to strengthen regionalism—a manifestation of individualism—through the purported autonomy of state and federal courts to interpret federal law itself. All of this reflects personalism and, in some cases, the desire to manipulate cases according to local interests, which just comes to show the latency of the old patrimonialism in a bizarre attempt to disguise the interest to benefit others under the guise of the "freedom to decide".

Personalism is clearly connected to a system that favours individual decisions over the decisions of the courts that represent institutional will, while patrimonialism can only survive in an irrational system, where cases are treated in a particularized fashion, without any regard to equality and legal certainty.

On the other hand, the individualistic and uncommitted perspective of a judge who believes that he is free to interpret the law clearly reflects personalism, as well as exaltation of autonomy and the complete lack of commitment to general and institutional goals.

4.6 Continuous Reproduction of the Old Slogan That the Judge Is Subject Only to the Law: An Excuse for Irrationality?

It is not uncommon to hear that judges should not respect supreme court precedent because they are subject only to the law. Obviously, this slogan can have two meanings: either it reveals a complete ignorance of the meaning of the law in a contemporary State, or, worse, it is genuine bad faith and intellectual dishonesty, designed to preserve the irrational exercise of judicial power in favor of those who benefit from it.

Idea that the judge is subject only to the law is associated with authoritarian periods in history, when the arbitrariness of government and the manipulation of institutions were the norm, such as during Getulio Vargas' dictatorship almost a century ago. As judicial decisions, during times of great populist fervour and of authoritarian wielding of power, are easily manipulated, including by the ideology of the dominant authority, the reactions to such periods underscore the independence of judges and subordinate the exercise of their power only to the law, seen as an expression of democratic will.

However, the evolution of interpretation theory, as well as the impact of constitutionalism itself—curiously, a reaction against legalistic authoritarianism—culminated in the disassociation between legal text and legal rule (interpretive result) as well as the incorporation of moral values contained in the rules of fundamental rights into decisional or interpretative reasoning, which not only led to the distinction between legislation and law, but also subjected the validity of the law to the constitution, bringing about a new kind of substantial legality. This clearly changed the concepts of law and adjudication. Basically, law stopped, once and for all, meaning legislation and adjudication no longer merely serves the will of the law (identified with legislation).

In this perspective, therefore, there is no way to accept that a judge may be subject simply to legislation. As the legal text is only the starting point from which the judge builds up his decision, given that it is impossible to interpret without evaluation and choice—either of interpretative directives or of one of the results of the interpretive activity—the decision assigns meaning to the legal text, thus constructing a legal rule. The judge works with the legislature to develop the law; he is no longer his servant, as, coherently, an adept of the idea that the judge is only subject to the law would have to admit.

As there is no longer any doubt that the interpreter may, from legitimate and reasonable interpretations, extract more than one rule from a single legal text, the need to give high courts the role of defining the law's assignable meaning emerges as mere logical consequence, without which, in fact, the legislators' own activity would never be completed. This role, as it is easy to see, is related to the need to have a coherent legal order that respects the spaces of freedom, the equitable distribution of the law and legal security. The law has shifted its place; it has abandoned the legal text—where, in fact, it never fully settled—and has taken the place of supreme court decisions. They, as mere logical consequence, began to represent the criteria that guide society and that solve disputes, giving rise to the practice we call precedent.

All this indisputably means that it is no longer tenable to say that judges and ordinary courts are subject only to the law and, therefore, cannot be bound by supreme court decisions. Judges, for the reason that they cannot rely on a legal text that, in principle, has several interpretations, can and must be bound by supreme court precedent. After all, to claim that the judge is subject only to the law, at the current stage of legal development, is to say that he is subject only to his own will or discretion.

That is why, if the old slogan is not supplanted by a rational grasp of the transformation of the concept of law, it can only be used in bad faith, to preserve a situation in which the judge has no commitment to the law and to the institution he belongs to, with the single aim of offering spoils to certain social positions, lawyers and judges who benefit from the irrationality of adjudication.

A system that gives authority to supreme court decisions and sees them as binding and mandatory precedents ensures the impartiality of adjudication in all echelons of the judiciary organization and, consequently, thwarts shrewdness (*jeitinho*) and lobbying, the practices of personal relationships and idiosyncratic of the Brazilian cultural constitution.

4.7 To Whom Does Irrationality Matter?

In a patrimonial and personalist culture, judges tend to treat identical cases differently. Obviously, this is not to accuse anyone of misconduct or anything of the sort. In the same way it has been argued, on a theoretical level, the need to guarantee the individual right to a day in court, that is, the right to adequately participate in proceedings—so that, consequently, obscurantism and arbitrariness are frustrated—it should be made clear, at this moment, that, in order to avoid the manipulation of judicial outcomes, it is imperative to give the proper and natural authority to supreme court precedents, thus removing from judges and ordinary courts the "option" of not taking them into consideration when deciding a case.

In fact, when we consider the reasons that conspire against the respect for supreme court precedents, it is impossible not to notice the obvious fact that a judge that does not adopt an impersonal standard of conduct cannot feel at ease in a system where there is a previous definition of decisional standards. Of course, in this case scenario, the leeway for subjectivity and, therefore, for judicial discretion is limited. At least as it concerns the application of the law, a judge cannot act in way that would favour any of the parties.

Evidently, precedent may be disregarded when the case under examination has particularities that distinguish it from the case that underpins the precedent in question. However, judges and courts have a heavy argumentative burden when they do not enforce a legal precedent that, according to the arguments made by one of the parties, is, in principle, binding upon the case.

Furthermore, a supreme court cannot refuse to apply a precedent when there are no reasons that justify overruling it. We should remember that disagreeing with a certain interpretation or solution given to a question of law is no opportunity to repeal precedent. Anyway, what matters is that logic of binding precedent prevents the manipulation of the decisions or favouritism towards one of the parties.

On the other hand, it is also true that lawyers may themselves not feel at ease in a system where the solution of cases cannot vary in what concerns the questions of law already decided by a supreme court. There is no doubt that they will be left with less space—if any—to defend the position of their clients.[40] This, however, unlike what a corporatist point of view may suppose in a debased defence of the profession, is absolutely rational and ethical.

[40] The lack of predictability, stemming from the absence of respect towards precedent, is a stimulus to cordiality and, therefore, to the proliferation of lobbyists disguised as lawyers.

Well, supreme courts exist precisely to give unity to the law, so that, after they have intervened and decided, lawyers have the onus to inform their clients about the court's precedent and explain to them the risks involved in prospective litigation. It falls to lawyers to warn clients of possible loss in filing a lawsuit or in resisting a sound claim filed against them, which stimulates settlements, thus inhibiting the expansion of litigation with all its nefarious consequences.

Add to that that it is neither rational, nor ethical—as should be obvious—to widen the share of available arguments to lawyers at the expense of judicial decisions becoming unpredictable. Predictability, besides being a natural result of the unity of law and of the due performance of supreme courts' constitutional role, is not only an element of great importance to optimize the administration of justice, but also necessary to develop society in an environment of respect towards the law.

This does not mean that there are no social groups interested in the lack of predictability, or rather, in an irrational distribution of justice. Certainly, some litigating parties are not concerned with predictability. They prefer to place their faith in the relationships of sympathy, esteem and personal influence, emulating the "cordial mentality" that define the people who, coming from patriarchal families, began to participate in the public sphere without abandoning old habits.

The trajectory of the "cordial man" begins when he realizes his difficulty in living in a rational and impersonal environment, where personal relationships do not matter to his integration into the social arena. His fear of this place leads him to use his affective demeanour to seduce and seek intimacy to reach his purposes. The apparent friendliness that characterizes him, obviously, cannot not provide any form of association or congregation, nor any form of respect for the law, since it reveals only an individual interest that, consequently, engenders repulsion towards any law that can counter it. The law, due to its impersonal nature, "is not for the cordial man"; he presupposes a world that, like a family, must be presided by personality and that, therefore, naturally allows him to dodge the rules that harm him.

Precisely, the cordial man is the antithesis of the idea that the law is equal for all and, as a mere consequence, the patrimonialism that was incorporated into Brazilian culture is completely averse to a coherent legal order and to a rational system of distribution of justice. Authoritarian governments, the most privileged social positions, the deformed environments of judgeship and of the legal profession, not only do not need predictability, but also do not want equality, and much less coherence and rationality. Hence, they pretend not to see the indispensability of a theory that enhances the authority of the role played by supreme courts.

4.8 Who Can Live with Irrationality?

There are litigants who can be described as "habitual", as opposed to those who only episodically engage in litigation, due to conflicts that may occur in their lives, who are called "eventual" litigants. The first are organizations that carry out activities that can reach large numbers of people, that enter into contracts *en masse*, and that, because of this, can frequently violate rights and cause harm. This distinction has been used by Cappelletti before to address the issue of the access to justice.[41]

Certainly, one cannot say that habitual litigants are interested in an irrational distribution of justice. They also rely, and *a lot*, on predictability. However, these litigants can get accustomed to a system that produces different decisions for identical cases. Given the multitude of lawsuits that habitual litigants have before courts, they can compensate one loss for a win in another case, balancing out their budgets according to business logic. On the other hand, eventual litigants, when they get unfavourable judgments, have no way to reverse their loss in another similar case.

Therefore, from the *exclusive viewpoint of the result of the lawsuit*, an eventual litigant takes on more risks to seek justice in a system devoid of the unity of law. In the event of an unfavourable judgment, it will be impossible to try again for a positive outcome, which is not the case of habitual litigants. That is why, besides the importance of identifying who benefits from a judicial system's irrationality, we must also consider who can endure it. After all, not everyone can afford to gamble on obtaining a favourable judgment in another case "left to chance" at the hands of the judiciary.

4.9 Fear of Giving Power to Supreme Courts?

On the other hand, something else, stemming from the origins and traditions of civil law, still underscores the difficulty in giving authority to supreme court precedent. In the setting of the French Revolution there was a feeling that courts, especially high courts, posed a danger to revolutionary power. There were compelling reasons to believe that courts could manipulate the law.[42] That is why the power of judges was mystically reduced to the description of the text of the law in Montesquieu's famous theory on the separation of powers.[43]

---

[41] Cappelletti (1974, 1988).

[42] In the period of absolute monarchy, judges faced the sovereign himself, taking on essentially legislative functions. In the battle between judges and the monarch, their weapon was the manipulation of the law, so that secular history also showed to the revolutionaries of France the need to preserve and protect the authority of the law against judicial bodies. See Marinoni (2019), p. 27.

[43] We should remember that, according to Montesquieu, the "power to judge" should be exercised through a purely intellectual activity, capable of only revealing the law as already produced by parliament. If the "power to judge" was not separated from the legislative, the power over the life and liberty of citizens would be arbitrary, because the judge would be a legislator. The "power to judge" is also limited by executive activity, which has the power to enforce its decisions. If it were not like this, judges would have the strength of oppressors. Given this, because it should be reserved for judges only the power to say what had already been said by the legislative, Montesquieu concluded that the "power to judge" was, in any way, a "null power" (*en quelque façon, nulle*). See Tarello (1976), pp. 192, 280.

Curiously, however, the natural evolution—which pervaded various periods of history—of the power of judges, which was also the result of the development of interpretation theory and of constitutionalist thought, was not enough to scare away the fear of giving authority to supreme court decisions. There are still those who think the power of courts can rival the law produced by parliament. And not only that; there is, in the social scene, a prevailing sentiment that courts can be weaponized by the executive against the legislative branch.

However, the power of the Superior Court of Justice to define the meaning of federal legislation and of the Supreme Federal Court to define the meaning of the constitution is not just something that flows naturally from the theoretical conclusion that the interpreter rebuilds the law, by evaluating and rationalizating over the legal text—the reason why judges cooperate with legislators to develop the law according to the needs of society—, as it is also anchored in the constitution, which gives these courts the duty to give "unity to the law" and, therefore, to "give meaning to the law".

This means that the authority of supreme court precedent not only cannot rival the power of parliament, to the extent that it naturally results from the development of interpretation theory and the evolution of the concept of law, as it is also indispensable to a coherent legal order, without which there is no legal security nor the possibility of equality before the law.

Moreover, the idea that supreme courts can be weaponized by government, by virtue of the president being responsible for appointing his ministers, equally does not hold against a closer inspection of the facts. In fact, when we consider excess powers being given to these courts, the problem should not only be in possible government pressure—because not only the president participates in the appointment process of a government minister, but also does the legislature and, in the case of the Superior Court of Justice, state and federal courts, the Public Ministry and the Brazilian Attorney Bar Association, depending on the case—but in the influence several sectors of society may exert therein.

It happens that if supreme courts can be influenced by government and organized groups, there is also a natural counterweight, inherent to the social reflection of the power wielded by a court of precedent. It is indispensable to remember that a court with this function, unlike courts of review and cassation, deals with legal issues that matter to society, that is, with a question of law that, once settled by precedent, will shine a light on social life and serve as a compass for other judges and courts to solve concrete cases.

This means that all of society has an interest in controlling the exercise of supreme court's powers, more than the parties involved in the dispute. To put it clearly, all those who may potentially be affected by the solution established in precedent have a concrete interest. The result of this is the procedure that allows the intervention of *amici curiae* before the Supreme Federal Court and the Superior Court of Justice.

The control of supreme court decisions should be done especially by the legal community, by lawyers and scholars, through criticism and discussions in books, reviews, newspapers, conferences and in classrooms, with the consequent repercussions on the media, particularly in cases of greater social relevance. A wrong decision will certainly be criticized by jurists, professors and lawyers and thus placed on the agenda of the academy and the Bar Association, whose functions are intimately related to the proper development of the law and, therefore, cannot turn off criticism of supreme court precedents.

References

Biéler A (2012) O pensamento econômico e social de Calvino. Cultura Cristã
Cadiet L, Normand J, Mekki SA (2013) Théorie Générale du Procès. PUF
Campante RG (2003) O patrimonialismo em Faoro e Weber e a sociologia brasileira. Revista de Ciências Sociais 46:162–194
Candido A (1995) O significado de "Raízes do Brasil". In: Raízes do Brasil (Sérgio Buarque de Holanda). Companhia das Letras
Cappelletti M (1974) Dimensioni della giustizia nelle società contemporanee. Il Mulino
Cappelletti M (1988) Acesso à justiça. Fabris
Chase O (2005) Law, culture, and ritual – disputing systems in cross-cultural context. New York University Press
Chiassoni P (2007) Tecnica dell'Interpretazione Giuridica. Il Mulino
Damatta R (1997) Carnavais, malandros e heróis. Rocco
Damatta R (2001) O que faz o brasil, Brasil? Rocco
Gerhardt MJ (2008) The power of precedent. Oxford University Press
Guastini R (2011) Interpretare e Argomentare. Giuffrè
Holanda SB (1995) Raízes do Brasil. Companhia das Letras
Holanda SB (2012) O homem cordial. Companhia das Letras
Kagan R (2001) Adversarial legalism – the American way of law. Harvard University Press
Levinson S (1988) Constitutional faith. Princeton University Press
Locke J (1980) Second treatise of government. Hackett
Marinoni LG (2019) O STJ enquanto Corte de Precedentes. Thomson Reuters
Martínez FR (2003) La ética protestante y el espíritu del constitucionalismo. Universidad Externado de Colombia
Portela A Jr (2012) Florestan Fernandes e o conceito de patrimonialismo na compreensão do Brasil. Revista do Programa de Pós-Graduação em Sociologia da USP 19:9–27
Rosenn KS (1998) O jeito na cultura jurídica brasileira. Renovar
Tarello G (1976) Storia della cultura giuridica moderna. Assolutismo e codificazione del diritto. Il Mulino
Tarello G (1980) L'Interpretazione della Legge. Giuffrè
Taruffo M (1975) La Motivazione della Sentenza Civile. Cedam
Weber M (2004a) Economia e sociedade. v. 1. Editora UnB
Weber M (2004b) Economia e sociedade. v. 2. Editora UnB
Weber M (2004c) A ética protestante e o espírito do capitalismo. Companhia das Letras
Wood GS (1998) The creation of the American Republic: 1776–1787. The University of North Carolina Press

Other Documents

Quental A (1871) Causes of decay of peninsular peoples in the last three centuries). Speech given in the premises of Casino Lisbonense in Lisbon on May 27, 1871, during the first Session of the Democratic Conference

Chapter 5
Justification for a System of Precedents

Contents

It is important to remember that the lack of authority of supreme court decisions derives not only from the theoretical rejection of the idea that supreme courts' decisions must guide other courts but also from the indifference of people holding significant social positions towards the rationalization of legal distribution within the country. This chapter seeks to demonstrate the importance of respecting precedents, especially to increase predictability and promote equality, economic rationality and personal responsibility.

5.1 Value and Behavior

The protagonists of a patrimonial culture, averse to impersonality, view the "generality of law" as a hindrance to the advancement of their aspirations. In such a culture, people do not feel obligated to behave according to the law and, therefore, aided by their relationships, seek to evade the laws that harm them. This is the territory of the "cordial man", a person unable to live within organizations and institutions characterized by rationality and impersonality.

L. G. Marinoni, *Culture and Predictability of Law*, SpringerBriefs in Law,
https://doi.org/10.1007/978-3-031-87161-0_5

There is a clear connection between the inability to coexist with impersonality—and, thus, with the generality of law—and the irrational distribution of justice. Everything that could compromise the uniform treatment of cases is welcomed by those who are interested in the prevalence of personal relationships. After all, the maxim that "like cases should be treated alike" is intolerable to those who feel entitled to have their claims treated in a individualistic way.

It is worth saying that if there is a clear association between the generality of law and the equal treatment of like cases, there is also a clear relationship between personality and irrationality in law enforcement. A patrimonialist culture not only disregards calculability or predictability but also benefits from a legal practice that jeopardizes rationality. Applying the same legal standard in different ways or deciding similar cases differently is something that is in line with this culture's logic.

The culture of the "cordial man" is not only disinterested in but, above all, fearful of a system of precedents. Such a culture does not see the unity of law, generality or even equality before the law as ideal or values. After all, the "cordial man" is a man of shrewdness, an expert in manipulation, a person devoid of any behavioural ethics and someone who does not care about strengthening institutions, predictability, rationality of conduct, economic rationalization and the benefits of a society where men are aware of their responsibilities.

A judicial system defined by respect for precedents is far more than a system equipped with mere technical features. Respecting precedents is a way to preserve the indispensable values of the rule of law, as well as to enable a way of living in which the law is embraced with dignity, in that, besides being applied equitably, it can determine behaviour and engender a way of life marked by personal responsibility.

5.2 Unity and Development of Law

A consequence of the development of interpretation theory is the greater or lesser indeterminacy of the interpretive results that can be elicited from the legal text. Hence the conclusion that, in a system where all judges interpret laws and review their constitutionality, it falls to supreme courts the task of defining the meaning of the law, as well as its validity. After the supreme court has ruled on an issue, by a logical consequence, no judge or court, even the supreme court itself, may resolve or decide a case without considering the established precedent. Only then there will no longer be uncertainty about the application of the law, which allows conscious behavior in compliance with it and the previous acceptance of responsibility, which is intrinsic to its violation.

Predictability, equality and other consequences, however, derive from the unity of law, i.e. from the establishment of precedent graced with authority. Precedent reveals something that is autonomous from legislation, the former is not merely a logical consequence of the latter. The reasons that explain the meaning given to the legal text, the declaration of the validity or invalidity, or the confirmation of one interpretation as valid over others certainly make up something that is embedded in a legal order of greater magnitude, comprised of laws and judicial precedents.

Unity of law results from a system of mandatory precedent and reflects a coherent legal system, enabling the predictability and uniform treatment of similar cases. Precedent, therefore, is a value in and of itself because it is indispensable for achieving the unity of law and ensuring the consistency of the legal order, both of which are conditions for the rationality of law.

In addition, a system of precedents favors the development of the law in a very positive and sophisticated way. There is no correlation between defining the meaning of the law and hindering its ripening; on the contrary, the power to assign meaning to the law carries with it the power to develop it. Precedent is not a sign of the calcification of the law but a symbol of its stability.[1] Courts, in fact, have the duty to overrule precedents that have been overtaken by societal evolution, superseded by a new general concept of law or, in exceptional cases, proved to be clearly wrong.

When a new case, different from that which gave rise to the precedent, demands from a judge the resolution of issues that have not been previously decided, it opens up an opportunity for the horizontal development of the law. To consider facts and legal questions related to the precedent, but that do not lead to its direct application, enables the development of issues alongside the one already settled, giving the law new contours or, more precisely, a wider profile that identifies a more complex reality.

This method of cultivating the law is far more sophisticated and effective than any other. When the law is expanded by embracing new realities, it undergoes a gradual and logical formative process. The solution of an issue related to precedent is a new step that cannot rebuff what has been originally decided. There is a relationship of continuity between the solution of the new issue and precedent, supplying adjudicators a way of thinking that flourishes gradually, akin to the reasoning of a scholar who continues to study a subject that encompasses many related questions that, therefore, can be considered over several essays or books. The most salient difference is that, in the case of precedent, the reasoning is not of one person, but of judges who, because they are part of an institution, must accept, without question, what has been defined by precedent, carrying on the court's discourse to solve a new issue. In other words, *ratio decidendi* or the decisive reasons are data in the discourse that is formed around the new issue.

An important decisional consistency, which contributes to the coherence of the law—although in a much different sense than the idea of consistency of the legal order defended once upon a time, wherein what matters is consistent application of the law. At this point, we are talking about consistency between two discourses or two precedents, which, because they complement each other, must remain coherent to ensure legal consistency. Consistency also requires that like cases be not treated differently, thus preventing the inconsistent application of the law.

---

[1] Alvim (2009).

5.3 Clarity and Generality

Unity of law contributes to clarity in the law, which is indispensable to guide social life and ensure predictability. The absence of clarity, understood as equivocality or indeterminacy of legal texts, is eliminated by precedent, which, by giving unity to law, erases the possibility of the same conduct being qualified in miscellaneous and unpredictable ways. This, undoubtedly, is necessary for men to behave freely and rationally under the rule of law and even to be able to trust the law and State action.

Likewise, precedent favor generality, to the extent that when there is unity of law, only one law regulates social life and is applied to everyone indiscriminately. The generality of the law, which is undermined by its equivocality and, especially, by the profusion of different judgments to equal cases, is remedied by precedent, which is applicable to all cases with the same circumstances, regardless of their social positions. This discourages shrewdness (*jeitinho*), the intervention of attorneys turned lobbyists and judicial partiality.

5.4 Promotion of Equality

Given the current state of Brazilian judicial practice, one notices that the idea that judges and courts can reach different decisions in identical cases is naturally accepted. It is even unsurprising when the same court decides like cases differently within a short period of time. In fact, judges do not seem to be even embarrassed when, faced with the workload reserved for them, they make decisions that are absolutely contradictory. For this reason, it has become commonplace to describe filing a lawsuit as a "lottery bet". Needless to say, this delegitimizes "justice". In this scenario, the judicial function is discredited, and the role of attorneys is diminished. Worse, it puts into question the impartiality of judges and the ethics of legal practice.

This irrational way of delivering justice was fostered by the idea that judges, because they have freedom to decide, need full autonomy and freedom to interpret the law. This way of thinking forgets that freedom to make judgment about the parties' arguments and evidence is not the same as freedom to say what the legal text means. Actually, this approach fails to see that freedom of conviction, essential to ensure independence and impartiality of judges, obviously cannot pretend to give them the ability to assign some meaning to the law that differs from that given by a supreme court that has been constitutionally empowered to define the meaning of the law.

We should note that it is the judiciary, not any and all judges in their own way, who works with the legislative in building the law. Judges take part in giving meaning to the law until the supreme court has the "final word". This is the logic of the institution and of the exercise of its power and authority. Indeed, if it were not so, the judiciary would only disrupt the consolidation of law, by creating multiple legal forms—applied to judges' liking—to regulate social life, an adventure that is still very welcome by bad judges, bad lawyers and by certain litigants.

It is curious to notice, however, how, despite the visible irrationality in adjudication across the country, it is still argued—rhetorically—that the jurisprudence of the Superior Court of Justice ensures the uniform interpretation of federal law by all state and federal courts. This assumption forgets that this uniformity can only be obtained by a court of cassation if it were theoretically true that laws have only one inborn rule, whose wrongful application by an ordinary court's decision would force the higher court to review it, in a constant come-and-go where supreme court decisions never have binding force and ordinary courts are always allowed to make mistakes.

But when we see that the supreme court gives meaning to the law, having the "final word" about its possible interpretation, and that this is an act that produces something autonomous from it, adding substance to the legal order, it also becomes clear that not only the unity of the law, but also equality before it, naturally calls for a mandatory or binding efficacy to supreme court decisions.

Binding efficacy is not an abstract requirement, desired by a particular way of understanding the law, but a consequence of equality. The same reason that led to the formulation of the statement that "all are equal before the law" is implicit in the need to have supreme court decisions as binding precedent. It is something indispensable in a country that really believes—and got tired of demagogically proclaiming—that everyone should be treated equally under the law.

5.5 Institutional Strengthening

The idea that the interpretation of the law and the resolution of questions of law is a "process", which begins before trial judges and appellate courts—who must solve disputes—and culminates in a supreme court—charged with assigning meaning to the law and developing it to make it suit reality—fosters or should foster in judges and justices a rational feeling that they share adjudicative power.

When we bear in mind that, within the echelons of the judiciary, judges, appellate courts and supreme courts have different functions, none of them interfering with the others, the respect of one judicial body towards the duties of the others becomes natural and rational. Obviously, there is no reason for appellate judges, for example, to feel without authority or freedom to judge their cases simply because they must follow a higher court's precedent, when they are aware that it is not up to them to precipitously give meaning to the law, but only to solve cases according to it, which includes the law pronounced by supreme courts.

Similarly, trial judges, though pressured by the needs of a different environment, would not fail to follow precedent, as they realize that the legitimate exercise of their function supposes respect to those of the supreme courts. We ought to remember, moreover, that supreme courts and state and federal courts should also respect the role of trial judges and not unduly meddle in their affairs.

Anyway, the knowledge that it is up to the supreme courts to determine the interpretation and the validity of laws begets the feeling in judges and lower courts that, when they follow precedent, they are sharing duties in the adjudicative process.

Therefore, the principles of unity of law and binding precedent strengthen the judiciary as an institution. Judges become aware that adjudication, to be realized adequately, depends on the combination of several and different functions. That is not what happens when they, in the name of a mythical and illusory "freedom" do judge in disagreement with supreme courts, give the law the meaning they deem most suitable.

5.6 Limitation of State Power

For men—especially those who work and invest in activities that are regulated by the State—to develop, they need to be able to place their trust in State action—whether administrative, legislative or judicial. The amount spent in energy and resources is inversely proportional to the lack of faith in State action. Not only the businessman, but also the "common man" needs guarantees that the State will not surprise him to be able to live peacefully.

However, when the law is devoid of clarity and the administration of justice produces results that cannot be calculated, citizens are left without any security or guarantee that they will not be hit with an unfair surprise. The plurality of judicial opinions over the same question of law curtails the safety that must govern relations between private people and the State, which in turn increases the burdens in contracts and investments.

Moreover, the indeterminacy of legal texts and the absence of a clear definition of the reasons that solve questions of law always gives the State the possibility, albeit unjustifiably, to pressure private parties. In public-private relations, predictability is much more important to an individual than to government. While the former depends on predictability, the State never hesitates to play with the absence of predictability to obtain arbitrary results.

All this implies that the limitation of State power by law, which is essential to democratic freedom and economic stability, in fact, depends on a system of binding precedents, that is, on a judicial system in which supreme courts exercise their function of determining the meaning and validity of laws.

5.7 Predictability

Predictability is essential for the rule of law. Individuals need to know the meaning of the actions they can take to live freely and self-develop.

Predictability effectively matters when one realizes that the same legal text can purport several interpretations or legal rules. The mere publication of the law, once seen as the guarantor of predictability, ceases to have any importance when one knows that a plurality of meanings can be taken out from one legal text. In this sense, all things considered, knowledge of legislated law becomes irrelevant.

This means that to obtain predictability there is no alternative but the unity of law, derived from the exercise of the function of supreme courts. A system that really cares about predictability cannot admit that, after a supreme court ruling on a given issue, the human behavior that is under its umbrella can be evaluated according to the flavour of cases and the opinion of each judge. Furthermore, it is recognized by an important civil law doctrine[2] not only that the law is not necessary to guarantee predictability, but that *stare decisis* is greatly effective at such.[3]

Predictability, besides avoiding surprises, allows people to trust in their rights. We know, therefore, that choosing one course of action not only will not result in something unexpected, as we are also assured that, given a certain situation, one or other right will be engendered that cannot be contested and thus can be fully exercised.

5.8 Economic Rationality

Economic rationality is closely linked to predictability. As seen earlier in this book, the Protestant asceticism, in Weberian terms, relied upon the calculability of the results of social actions, in turn necessary for the a rational organization of life guided by religious values. Calculability, or predictability, constitutes an assurance that actions and conduct are able to meet the goals pursued by the believers in the dependence between the proof of their salvation and an inner-worldly way of life. The search for signs of election, which stem from the acts of daily life, especially work done with care and quality, had a strong influence on the development of capitalism and culminated in the need for a clear and predictable law.

Thus, predictability has always been indispensable to life endowed with rationality and also to the development of capitalism. Therefore, the profusion of miscellaneous judicial decisions, by suggesting the absence of criteria for entrepreneurs to define their strategies of action and investment, certainly conspires against the economy.

Predictability allows the definition of expectations by entrepreneurs and thus contributes to the optimization of investments and the rationalization of expenses with organization and raw materials, which also enables adequate compensation of workers. Investments, in the absence of predictability, become more onerous and less efficient, hindering business growth.[4]

---

[2] Corsale (1979), p. 36.

[3] Arthur Goodhart's famous essay presented the idea that legal certainty is the most important cause for the institution of stare decisis of for the establishment of a system of binding precedent. Goodhart (1934), p. 40.

[4] Lee (2000), p. 652: "The cost savings associated with a system of stare decisis extend beyond those incurred in litigation. Increased certainty not only discourages litigation; it also enables more efficient planning in reliance on precedent. Again, compare the effects of the current system of

Moreover, economic rationality requires the protection of trust. The trust in government action is essential for economic investment and for energy expenditure on important projects for the country's development. Acts of breach of trust, which inevitably become known to potential investors, obviously inhibit new initiatives. So, when an economic project is grounded on precedent, there is need for caution in modulating the temporal effects of any decision that overrules it.

In the case of companies that sign contracts or determine investment strategies, expenses etc., based on precedent, there is no way to conclude that, in the face of its overruling, the actions that were taken under its rule can be struck down. We must determine whether, at the time of action, there was "justified trust" in precedent, or if, on the contrary, precedent was worn out and thus could not have supported social action. If, at the time of action, there was justified trust in precedent, because a supreme court had not signalled the loss of its authority or there was no clear critique in academia about its fragility, the invalidation of acts founded on precedent constitutes an "unfair surprise", which is inconceivable in a system that acknowledges that precedent records the meaning of the law and guides society on how to proceed.

We should remember, for example, that until August 2004 the Brazilian Superior Court of Justice constantly recognized the right to tax credits in taxation over industrialized products, created by article 1 of Decree-Law 491/1969. The Court, in a hearing held in June of 2007, heard argument in a case (EDiv in REsp 738.689) that sought the recognition of this right, but upholding a decision that it had made in August of 2004, which struck down the right to tax credits, it denied the possibility to give non-retroactive effects to the 2004 decision in order to protect the use of tax credits by taxpayers made until August 2004. However, a dissenting opinion warned that only taxpayers who sued until August 2004, and they alone, had the expectation of a favourable judgment. They used tax credits at a time when the Court held a strong position in their favour. This use implied the reduction of costs and prices charged by these companies, corresponding to the amount of money subtracted from owed taxes, leading them to guide their plans and activities based on that reality. These are the acts of taxpayers, having and using tax credits before a jurisprudential shift, that were perfected under the 'shadow of legality' and now deserve to be preserved.[5]

This is one of the first instances of judicial protection of citizen trust in supreme court decisions and therefore deserves its due attention. The protection of trust in supreme court precedent is crucial not only to ensure the fulfilment of rights, but also to enable rationality in life projects, including economic ones.

---

stare decisis, which establishes some barriers to self-reversal by the Supreme Court, to a more freely discretionary regime. The current system reduces the degree of upheaval in the Court's body of precedent, thus enabling 'the political branches and the people' more efficiently to 'plan against the background of known rules'. A more discretionary system, by comparison, would make planning and reliance more costly and less efficient". See Kaplow (1986), pp. 509–617.

[5] STJ, EREsp n. 738.689/PR, Relator: Min. Teori Albino Zavascki, 22.10.2007. (Herman Benjamin, Min., dissenting).

5.9 Respect for the Law and Personal Responsibility

The uncertainty about the interpretation of a legal text or about the solution of a question of law dilutes the sense of personal responsibility. No individual would feel responsible for his conduct when there is doubt about its illegality. When the State itself, through the branch entrusted with the enforcement of the law, is shown to be insecure and contradictory, it becomes impossible to develop a social conscience based on the feeling of responsibility or the respect for the law.

A life based on law, wherein individuals feel responsible for their conduct, presupposes an identifiable law, which leaves no room for doubt and, therefore, for personal reasons of absolution. Contradictory decisions deprive the law of authority, that is, they deny the law its intrinsic force to stimulate and avoid behaviors and, thus, its ability to make men feel responsible. There is no doubt that any penalty, when applied without any commitment to the unity of the law, looks more like discretion than accountability, but the most serious consequence of this, when we consider responsibility as ethics of behaviour, is that no one can guide their life based on a law that cannot be identified or that is applied by courts so contradictorily.

It is interesting to note that, as demonstrated by Weber,[6] Protestant asceticism harbored a way of life in which everyday actions, particularly those linked to the performance of work, should in susbstance dignify God. Especially Calvinists, believers in the doctrine of predestination of men, felt embarrassed to make introspective assessments to verify whether they were actually behaving as elected. This demand of man by himself according to biblical ideas engendered a personal responsibility with enormous weight, in which the roles of accuser, defender and judge are vested in a single person. Protestant ethics, beyond turning work into a religious duty, had a great impact on personal responsibility, so much so that it is possible to mistake Protestant behaviour with the behaviour based on an almost unbearable personal responsibility.[7]

One might wonder what this has to do with behaviour guided by the law. We should make clear that a life based on law is obviously far different from the behaviour of the man who lives so as not to be reached by it. The latter, instead of giving value to a life based on law, is solely interested in enjoying life so as not to be surprised by it. Calvinists, for sure, were afraid of not being saved, but lived according to the precepts of the Bible, convincing themselves—and no one else—to feel worthy before God. The man who decides to have a life based on the law is not worried about not being sanctioned, rather he wants to live in accordance with it due to a moral and personal imperative. He adopts a way of life that, to be worthy of *himself*, must align with the State rules that regulate social life.

---

[6] Weber (2004). See supra Chap. 1.

[7] Pound (1911), p. 819: "A fundamental proposition from which the Puritan proceeded was the doctrine that man was a free moral agent with power to choose what he would do and a responsibility coincident with that power. He put the individual and individual judgment in the first place".

It turns out that a life in conformity with the law and consequently permeated by responsibility is only viable in a State that protects the coherence of the legal order. The multiplicity of different decisions for the same cases undermines the posture of respect towards the law, which weakens or melts away the sense of responsibility of individuals.

Even when we think of the advantages of following the law for fear of punishment, it is clear that, the more diverse are the decisions concerning a question of law, the lower the burden of psychological pressure on the individual. Here it no longer matters if men may ethically guide their conduct, but only if the law has the ability to inhibit behavior and, thus, if it has authority to make itself be respected.

There is no doubt that the law loses authority in direct proportion to its indeterminacy. The fluidity of the meaning of the law conspires against its authority and may remove its power to regulate social life. The law, as a threat, is much less effective the more it provides an opportunity to think of it as unenforceable. In this sense, of course, the authority of the law to avoid the distortion of social behavior collapses. We should note, in fact, that even though individuals may feel constrained by the meaning given by courts to the law, it is still possible that they prefer not to comply with it to take on the risk of its eventual application.

Therefore, to lead a life based on law and for it to have enough strength to regulate life, it is fundamental to have unity of law and, therefore, that supreme courts function as courts of precedent. The individualization of law, essential to its authority, contributes to the flourishment of personal responsibility, although in different ways, in any of these cases.

References

Alvim TA (2009) Estabilidade e adaptabilidade como objetivos do direito: civil law e common law. Revista de Processo 172:121–174

Corsale (1979) Certezza del diritto e crisi di legittimità. Giuffrè

Goodhart AL (1934) Precedent in English and Continental law. Law Q Rev 50:40–62

Kaplow (1986) An economic analysis of legal transitions. Harv Law Rev 99:509–617

Lee TR (2000) Stare decisis in economic perspective: an economic analysis of the Supreme Court's doctrine of precedent. North Carolina Law Rev 78:643–706

Pound R (1911) Puritanism and the common law. Am Law Rev 45:811–829

Weber M (2004) A ética protestante e o 'espírito' do capitalismo. Companhia das Letras

Case Law

STJ, EREsp n. 738.689/PR, Relator: Min. Teori Albino Zavascki, 22.10.2007. (Herman Benjamin, Min., dissenting)

The manufacturer's authorised representative in the EU is Springer Nature Customer Service Centre GmbH, Europaplatz 3, 69115 Heidelberg, Germany. If you have any concerns regarding our products, please contact ProductSafety@springernature.com

Printed and bound by CPI Group (UK) Ltd, Croydon, CR0 4YY
30/09/2026
02225468-0004